Getting Started with Jesus

The Basics of Christian Living for Believers

Second Edition

Olivia Jones

ISBN 979-8-89243-992-3 (paperback)
ISBN 979-8-89428-041-7 (hardcover)
ISBN 979-8-89243-993-0 (digital)

Christian Faith Publishing
832 Park Avenue
Meadville, PA 16335
www.christianfaithpublishing.com

Printed in the United States of America

Now to Him who is able to keep you from stumbling,
And to present you faultless
Before the presence of His glory with exceeding joy,
To God our Savior,
Who alone is wise,
Be glory and majesty,
Dominion and power,
Both now and forever.
Amen.

—Jude 1:24–25

Second Edition Note

Getting Started with Jesus was the first book that I published back in 2012. Since then, publishing options have improved and increased, and I have gained more writing experience. In this version, I made a few edits to simplify or clarify language and moved a chapter. I hope these updates make it easier to read and understand. The content is generally the same as in the first edition, and I am a witness that it remains true.

Contents

Preface

I had the privilege of sharing my faith with a coworker recently. She expressed interest and, at the end of our discussion, asked, "How do I get started?" I gave her a brief answer, but her question continued to replay in my mind.

Having been a Christian for practically all my life, I assumed that everyone knew how to begin a relationship with the Lord. But how is a person supposed to know? Often, new believers begin by buying a Bible and trying to read it. But when the language is unclear or is difficult to understand because of varying translations or interpretations, they'll put it down. New believers might also decide to turn over a new leaf and try to live a perfect life. Within a day or two, they realize that it's too hard, and they stop trying. It doesn't take long for them to give up on Christianity altogether—a sad and unfortunate choice.

But there is good news! As with any new relationship, getting it started and developing it are the work and responsibility of both parties. In the case of Christianity, it's all about building a personal relationship with God. And guess what, God sought *you* out first to build a relationship with *you*. A humbling thought, isn't it? You don't have to chase after Him or persuade Him to desire a relationship with you as you often have to do with people. Moreover, He is delighted that you have freely chosen to enter into a relationship with Him.

I wrote this book to help you on the path of building a relationship with God and to share how you can begin living your life as a member of His holy family. We'll start by answering a few questions that you may have.

Am I getting started with Jesus or with God?

After reading the prior paragraph, you might be asking why I'm writing about getting started with God when the title of the book is *Getting Started with Jesus*. Today, people use the word *god* in many religions and have bestowed it on manmade objects that they worship in place of the true and living God. However, in the Christian faith, Jesus is still the name recognized as the only biological Son of God. So the title was chosen to make it clear to potential readers that the focus of this book is Jesus Christ and Christianity and not on other belief systems.

It is through Jesus that we become Christians and gain access to God the Father and the Holy Spirit. Jesus is a part of the Holy Trinity and is one with the Father. If you have accepted Jesus as your Savior and Lord and you believe that He died for your sins, rose from the dead, and has been preparing a wonderful place for you to live eternally, this book is for you. This book is also for those who are curious about what it means to be a Christian and to live the Christian lifestyle.

Is this book just for new Christians?

Many people have accepted Jesus as their Savior but have never sought a personal relationship with Him. Perhaps they thought it wasn't possible, didn't think it was necessary, or planned to get to know Him later. Some have attended church for decades but have felt something lacking in their relationship with God. So this book isn't only for those who consider themselves to be new Christians. It is for anyone who wants to get to know God better and to live the rest of their lives with and for Him.

Is this book for a specific religious group?

This book was not written for a particular Christian denomination—such as Baptist, Catholic, Reformed, Methodist, or Pentecostal. The topics covered in these pages are based on the scriptures set forth in the sixty-six books of the protestant Bible. That being said, the premise is that as Christians, we strive to live for God and not for a denomination, a church, or a pastoral leader.

Will this book tell me everything I need to know?

No. God gave us the Bible for that. The sole purpose of this book is to share the basics of living a Christian life as presented to us in God's Word. It was written to help you calibrate your compass so that you can travel in the right direction. You will build on the knowledge you gain by reading and studying the Bible, listening to the Word preached in sermons, participating in Bible studies, and revelation from the Holy Spirit. You'll also learn and grow through your life experiences and through the testimonies of other believers.

British evangelist, pastor and author Alan Redpath wisely stated, "The conversion of a soul is the miracle of a moment, but the manufacture of a saint is the task of a lifetime." You entered the manufacturing plant when you accepted Jesus Christ. So think of this book as your introductory course, Saint Manufacturing 101. The Bible is the full user manual that you will read and refer to for the rest of your life.

Let's get started

When I started writing this book, I imagined that you approached me, told me the good news that you accepted Christ as your Savior, we hugged, I congratulated you, and then you asked the question: "What happens next?"

I said, "I'd love to help you with that. Can we meet for about fifteen minutes for eleven days on a schedule that works for you?"

"Sure," you said. "But why?"

"To help you get started with Jesus."

You thought about it and then said, "I figured I'd just buy a Bible and start going to church."

"Yes, that's one way. But you can get off to a stronger start if you have a coach—you know, like a runner. You can certainly just go for it. But an experienced runner and coach can help you prepare properly."

You agreed, and now you're ready to begin.

The suggested approach for reading this book is to pick it up, go to your favorite reading spot, and read one chapter. Think about what you read and what it means for you. Write any thoughts or questions on the notes page at the end of each chapter. When you have an opportunity, discuss them with your pastor, Bible class teacher, or a trusted Christian friend. After you've taken time to think about the chapter, move on to the next and continue this process through the end of the book.

When you finish *Getting Started with Jesus*, I hope that you will be deeply committed to loving, knowing, and pleasing God. The most wonderful and satisfying relationship in my life is the one that I have with Him. I wish the same for you.

Chapter 1

Surrender Control of Your Life

Every way of a man is right in his own eyes.

—Proverbs 21:2a

Thinking back on my teenage years, I remember how anxious my friends and I were about reaching adulthood. We couldn't wait! Once we became adults, we'd be our own bosses. We wouldn't have to follow our parent's rules, and we'd be free to experience the world.

At the appropriate time, I received my much-awaited freedom. It didn't take me long to realize that adulting was not what I expected it to be. Freedom, it turned out, was a lot harder than it looked from the eyes of a child. From a child's eyes, freedom meant doing what you want when you want because you want with no one being able to tell you no. But from the adult perspective, it meant making my own decisions and benefiting or suffering from the resulting consequences. It also required that I have a job so that I could pay the rent, buy food, and purchase my own clothes. The job had rules, and I had new a boss. The boss told me what time to be at work, what to do while I was there, and what time I could leave. Needless to say, freedom was quickly redefined for me.

Eventually, most of us accept the shock that leaving our parents' homes requires being responsible for meeting our own needs. We settle into our newfound freedom and begin to morph into the adults that we will ultimately become. We set goals and design our lives based on what we think we know, what we see, what we've heard, what we have learned (right or wrong), and what we want to obtain or achieve in life.

At some point, we realize that we don't know enough to live successfully on our own. So we augment our knowledge by seeking and following the direction of others whom we feel are wiser than we are. We may follow the guidance and example of financial advisers, career managers, fashion designers, family members, neighbors, and friends. We then build our lives pursuing our goals—be they positive, negative, life-building, or life-diminishing.

In the midst of our establishing, pursuing, and achieving our goals, we realize that we still want more out of our lives. An inner voice tells us that there is more to life than this. We begin to wonder what's missing, and therein lies the problem. When we were being raised in our parents' homes, they were responsible for guiding us, providing for our needs, and directing our paths. We decided (or were told) that when we left their homes, we were to assume the responsibilities that our parents had and take care of ourselves. We were wrong.

We were wrong, and many of us never realized it. We sought to design our lives and establish our goals as if we had created ourselves. Consider this clearly fictional but relevant example: Imagine a family of rare, exquisitely crafted stringed instruments. The craftsman made each member of the family to achieve a specific purpose but did not disclose that purpose to the instruments early on. The viola becomes of age and decides that she wants to be an acoustic guitar. She has been influenced by the world of popular music, which acclaims the acoustic guitar to be a highly valued instrument. Viola likes the idea of being among celebrities, the rich and famous, and receiving the attention from the crowd that a solo acoustic guitar commands.

So she associates with the guitars and tries to mimic what they do. She cannot reshape herself, but she can modify her sound somewhat. Viola achieves a reasonable measure of success in her efforts but knows in her heart that something is missing, misaligned. She has four choices. She can ignore the feeling and continue living her life as a guitar. She can choose a different goal, such as becoming a cello, like her brother. She can quit altogether and rest on a shelf somewhere, never to contribute to the musical world again. Or she can ask the designer to reveal the purpose for which she was made.

Let's assume that she chooses the latter. Imagine her surprise when she learns that she was meant to be a viola. Imagine the joy that she'll feel the first time she is used for her intended purpose. Imagine that she obtains and follows instructions from her designer on how to properly care for herself. Think about how the designer can then guide her life and bless the world with beautiful music through her. Think about it.

We are designed by God

As unique beings, each of us was designed by God to be a blessing to this world. Although we may find a purpose and achieve a measure of success without God (or so it may seem), we will eventually feel an emptiness and lack of fulfillment if we are not realizing God's purpose for our talents and skills.

The Christian teacher Ravi Zacharias tells the true story of an extremely wealthy man from China who had achieved tremendous success in life. After accomplishing a very significant goal, he was surprised to find that he still felt that something was missing. Did he need more property, more women, more children, or more businesses? One day, the man agreed to attend a church service, and he heard about God. When he heard the good news of Jesus Christ, he realized that he had found the missing link.[1] It didn't cost him any money. Yet it was priceless and more valuable than any of his possessions.

Understand that no matter how smart, connected, and successful we are (or aren't) and no matter how wise our advisors, we all suffer from the same deficiency. We all have limited wisdom, foresight, and power. All of our hearts need and desire love, and God is love. We all need God. We were created by Him and for Him. In those ways, we were all created equal. God made us with needs and deficiencies because He desires a relationship with us and wants us to rely on Him.

When you accepted Jesus Christ as your Savior, you chose a different way of living. You accepted Jesus's payment for your sins, but you were to also give up being your own boss and directing your own life. Living for God affects every area of your life. Here is a key Bible verse that you should memorize:

> Trust in the Lord with all your heart and do not lean on your own understanding. In all your ways, acknowledge Him and He shall direct your paths. (Proverbs 3:5–6)

From now on, instead of trusting in people who are prone to fail you, make the decision to trust in God. He is all knowing, all powerful, and everywhere at all times. He will never leave or abandon you. He is never wrong and is incapable of making a mistake. His guidance never becomes outdated. He is the one to know. He is the best connection. He can never be replaced as the Creator and Master of the universe. You can completely trust God with your life.

As you develop your relationship with Him, there will be many times when you won't understand or can't see what He is doing. Continue to trust Him even when life doesn't make sense to you. By design, we have limited knowledge. We cannot know the mind of God. Eventually, you will come to understand that He is always in control.

The third line of the verse tells us to acknowledge God in all of our ways. We should not compartmentalize God by allowing Him only to control certain parts of our lives to the exclusion of others. We are to allow Him to be lord over every aspect of our lives and to guide us in every decision. The reward for trusting in God (even when we don't understand) and surrendering control to Him is that He will guide our lives perfectly. That is awesome!

The God who created the trees, oceans, the sun, the moon, the wind, the land, and the sky—the one who designed our bodies in our mother's wombs—is willing to guide our lives every day. Isn't that wonderful? When an astronaut sees a picture of the earth from space, he can't see individual human beings. But God knows exactly where we are at every single moment of our existence. It is amazing that He knows us so well and loves us so much.

Live with freedom

The starting point for building a relationship with God is accepting Jesus Christ as your Savior and turning over control of your life. Acknowledge that you were created by the Master Designer for a reason. No matter where you are in your life right now, your goal from this point forward should be to allow God to use you for His purposes.

While you may be a little nervous about giving up control, you should feel a new sense of freedom instead. This is the *real* freedom, and it is liberating to think about it. You no longer have to rely on yourself or others for the right answers and the right timing. You can rely on and rest in God. If He says it's right, it's right. If He says it's wrong, it's wrong. Pastor Charles Stanley often said, "Obey God, and leave all the consequences to Him." Doesn't that sound like freedom? It does to me.

Starting today, take time to reflect on your life:

- Do you know who you are?
- How have you made decisions in the past?
- Which of them are you proud of?
- Which do you regret?
- What future plans do you have?

If you want, write the answers on a piece of paper. When you have finished, ball it up and throw it in the trash. The Bible tells us in 2 Corinthians 5:17 (NLT) that "anyone who belongs to Christ has become a new person. The old life is gone; a new life has begun." So from this day forward, decide that you will give yourself to God, your designer. Let His plans become your plans. Let His goals become your goals. Trust God, and be free.

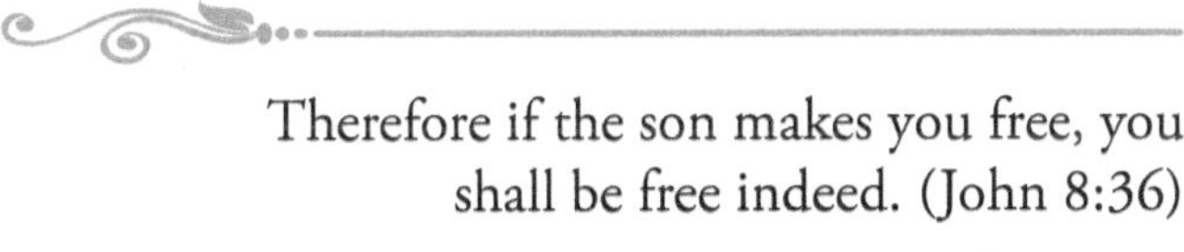

Therefore if the son makes you free, you
shall be free indeed. (John 8:36)

Chapter 2

Meet Satan—Your New Enemy

Stay alert! Watch out for your great enemy, the devil. He prowls around like a roaring lion, looking for someone to devour.

—1 Peter 5:8 (NLT)

Allowing God to guide and control your life is definitely the best decision you will have ever made. Please know that it will also be your most challenging decision. There are two reasons for this. First, change can be hard. You were the captain of your ship. You charted your course and knew where you were headed—or thought you knew. Now you have to give up control, deny what you want, and follow God's way.

God does not fully disclose His plans to us or give us a detailed road map in advance. We have to live by faith, trusting His guidance day by day. The other reason that your life with Christ will be challenging is because you have a new enemy. His name is Satan, also known as the devil.

Who is Satan?

As human beings, we live in a natural world in which we are able to physically see and touch things. It's difficult for most of us to understand angels and spiritual forces that we cannot see. Nevertheless, it is important that we understand that they exist. There is much more happening in this world through unseen forces than there is by those that we can see. For example, you have a body, a soul, and a spirit. We can see your body, but it can do nothing without your soul and spirit—both of which are invisible. There are spirits in this world, good and bad, who exist without human bodies like ours.

Satan is one of them. He is a powerful spiritual being who does not have a physical body of his own, but he is present and active on this earth. In the arts, cartoons, and movies, Satan is often presented as a devilish character who wears a bright-red suit, has horns, and carries a pitchfork. More modern works have given him a handsome human body with special powers. Know that he is an invisible spirit, and he has an army of demonic angels and evil humans who help him carry out his work.

Where did he come from?

According to the Bible, Satan was an angel in heaven at one time. Here is what it says:

> How you are fallen from heaven, O Lucifer, son of the morning! How you are cut down to the ground, You who weakened the nations! For you have said in your heart: I will ascend into heaven, I will exalt my throne above the stars of God; I will also sit on the mount of the congregation On the farthest sides of the north; I will ascend above the heights of the clouds, I will be like the Most High. Yet you shall be brought down to Sheol, To the lowest depths of the Pit. (Isaiah 14:12–15)

Satan, also known as Lucifer, was created by God and was described in the book of Ezekiel as having been the "seal of perfection, full of wisdom and perfect in beauty" (Ezekiel 28:12). He was the ordained and anointed mighty guardian angel who had "access to the holy mountain of God." Satan was blameless in all he did until evil was found in his heart (Ezekiel 28:14–15 NLT).

As we read the verses in Isaiah, we learn that Satan began to bask in his own glory and wanted to have more power and a higher position than God had given him. He wanted to become God's equal. But God can have no equal, so Satan was thrown out of heaven. Jesus said, "I saw Satan fall like lightning from Heaven" (Luke 10:18).

Although Satan cannot rule in heaven, he makes every effort to rule on this earth. Beginning with the first humans, Adam and Eve, Satan has desired to have human beings become his followers to carry out his work and to spend eternity with him in "the pit"—which is hell. If he can accomplish this, he'll feel that he has achieved equality with God.

Unfortunately for us, Satan is completely evil. Jesus tells us that Satan's desire is to "steal, kill, and destroy" (John 10:10). This makes him the exact opposite of God, who loves us and desires to give us a rich and fulfilling life. Following Satan means living on a path that leads to your destruction and being used to destroy others. It also means that you will spend eternity with him in hell, instead of in heaven with God. Eternity—as in now and forever.

Satan knows that if we know the truth about him and his evil desires toward us, we will not follow him. So he fools us through false advertisements. He tells us that what is bad is good, what is true is false, and what is right is wrong. He knows that because God gave humans free will—the right and ability to choose good or evil—he has a chance to draw us away and keep us away from God. That, my friend, is his goal. He plays dirty and will like to deliver a knock-out punch separating you from God as early in your life as possible and for as long as possible.

Before we allow God to guide our lives, Satan is pretty sure that we are on his team. This is because if we are not seeking guidance from God, Satan is able to guide us through his sources, which might be social media, influencers, television, games, movies, books, magazines, family, and friends. Some of those who we respect and listen to may be followers of God, but it's highly possible that many of them are not.

As long as Satan has the ability to persuade you and keep you away from God, he is happy. You see, he is always your enemy, but before you accepted Christ, you were not a threat to his plan. So he didn't have to pay much attention to you. But when you accepted Jesus and chose to live for God, Satan felt rejected and defeated.

He realizes that as you grow closer in your relationship with and your commitment to God, you'll move farther away from him. You'll learn the truth about him (and about God), he'll have one less follower, and you'll make a positive difference in your circle of influence. He also knows that if you allow God to use you for His purpose, you will have the ability to do wonderful things for God during your lifetime.

What can you expect from Satan?

Because you are a follower of God, expect Satan to use every trick in the book to keep you from knowing God and to discourage you from living for Him. God gives us many examples throughout the Bible of ways that Satan works. God also gives us many examples of how He helps His people overcome anything that Satan tries to do. Although it will be hard at times to live God's way in a world that seems to prefer the opposite, remember that God's way is *always* the right way. Living for God leads to a fulfilling life. Satan's way (ungodly living) may be advertised as life, but it ends in death—death of relationships, death of hope, and death of freedom.

As you move forward in building your relationship with God, live with your eyes open. Notice the difference between those who truly live for God and those who don't. Followers of God have a level of contentment, peace, and joy that others do not. It comes from the wisdom that God gives us through his Word, His love for us, and His great care of us. Yes, we have to battle Satan and our natural desire to follow him. But it's well worth it. No matter how powerful he is and how many people he has on his side (typically the physical majority), God's power far exceeds Satan's. God has full control over Satan.

Beware of your new enemy. Resist Satan and follow God.

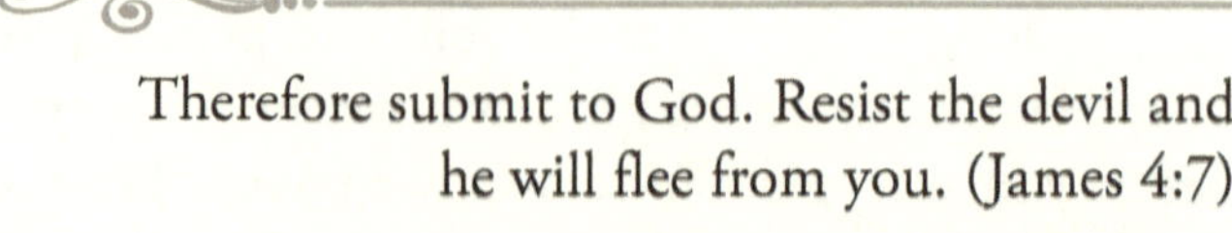

Therefore submit to God. Resist the devil and
he will flee from you. (James 4:7)

Thoughts, Reflections, and Questions

Chapter 3

Meet Your Helper— God's Holy Spirit

And I will pray the Father, and He will give you another
Helper, that He may abide with you forever.

—John 14:16

Many professional athletes have suffered shame and penalties over the years for being caught using steroids. Possible reasons that they turned to the supplements are fear of inadequacy, stiff competition for their positions, a desire to stop the hands of time from taking a toll on their athletic prowess, or perhaps even greed. The general consensus is that what they did was wrong. However, each of them has something in common with Christians: we believe that we need help beyond ourselves to reach our full potential. They allowed Satan to direct them to the wrong source. Christians look to God, the true source.

We're not looking for help to achieve fame, fortune, or a worldly prize. We seek help to live right before God. It's in our nature to sin, to have wrong thoughts, chase after wrong things, and make choices that lead to self-destruction. The Bible tells us this:

When you follow the desires of your sinful
nature, the results are very clear: sexual immo-

> rality, impurity, lustful pleasures, idolatry, sorcery, hostility, quarreling, jealousy, outbursts of anger, selfish ambition, dissension, division, envy, drunkenness, wild parties, and other sins like these. Let me tell you again, as I have before, that anyone living that sort of life will not inherit the Kingdom of God. (Galatians 5:19–20)

You may question the accuracy of verse 19 because you know people who you feel are "naturally" good and would never do those things. It's a rare person who would commit the sins in the entire list, but everybody was born with an inclination to do wrong. No matter how good a person may appear, he or she has something inside that can lead to self-destruction or have a negative impact on others.

It could be a physical vice such as alcoholism, an emotional issue such as low self-esteem, or excessive fear. It may not have made the top ten sin list and may not even be evident to others, but it's there. It is displeasing to God and often too strong for them to overcome completely on their own. This is true for *all* of us.

Satan's goal is to latch on to our natural desires and weaknesses and introduce regular opportunities for us to stumble and remain in sin. While were there, he reminds us of our sinfulness and worthlessness with the hope that we'll never rise above it. He wants to be there "till death do us part"—but we won't part. He'll pull us into an eternal hell with him.

Without Christ, we would be hopeless, and hell would be our end. But thank God for Jesus. He knew that in this world we would have struggles both on the inside and outside of ourselves. While living on earth as a man, Jesus showed us how to resist temptation, how to live, and how to love. But He didn't stay here in a physical form. And He doesn't come back in the flesh to walk among every generation. Nevertheless, He knew that every one of us would need Him every day, so He sent us a Helper. Jesus said this:

> If you love Me, keep My commandments. And I will pray the Father, and He will give you another

> Helper, that He may abide with you forever—the
> Spirit of Truth, whom the world cannot receive,
> because it neither sees Him nor knows Him: but
> you know Him, for He dwells in you and will be
> in you. I will not leave you orphans: I will come
> to you. (John 14:15–18)

Who is the Holy Spirit?

When I was a child attending church, my friends and I would see people praising God excitedly, and we'd say that they "caught the Holy Ghost!" That was how we defined the Holy Spirit during our immature Christian years, and we looked forward to the day when we'd "catch" it like that. I later learned that the Holy Spirit isn't something that we should look for in that manner.

Throughout the Bible, we read stories that give us insight into who the Holy Spirit is and how He works. We meet Him in the first Bible book, Genesis, which tell us this:

> In the beginning God created the heavens and
> the earth. The earth was formless and empty,
> and darkness covered the deep waters. And the
> Spirit of God was hovering over the surface of the
> waters. (Genesis 1:1-2 NLT)

This passage tells us that the Holy Spirit (Spirt of God) was with God in the beginning. He was there when the earth was formed. He was there when mankind was created. The Holy Spirit is a part of God and is given to us by God.

Throughout the Old Testament, there are many exciting stories that tell how the Spirit of God helped people to carry out important tasks. His help came through wisdom and insights, special talents and abilities, and increased courage and strength. These stories tell us that the Holy Spirit has power and authority to carry out God's plans.

I think of the Holy Spirit as the part of God that He deploys. He can split into an infinite number of parts yet maintain complete power to fulfill God's will. That's incredible. What's even more awesome is that because you are a believer, God sent His Holy Spirit to live within you (John 14:16). We have something extra on the inside that unbelievers do not have or understand. Our bodies are temples of the Holy Spirit (1 Corinthians 6:19). This should affect how we view ourselves as children of God and how we treat our bodies.

The Holy Spirit is also God's seal on His people. The seal sets us apart from this world, and we are identified as part of God's holy family. As we mature in our faith and allow God to lead us through His Spirit, we'll begin to look like our Father and reflect His character.

What does the Holy Spirit do?

Imagine being in school and taking a very important class. It is critical that you pass the class, but you can't do it by yourself. You're willing, but you don't think you're smart enough. Fortunately, you have a rich father who can provide you with all the help you need to be successful. He sends you a helper who is with you twenty-four seven to support you in every way. Your helper is a tutor and a counselor, and because no one can see him but you, he calls to your mind what you studied during your tests. As a result, you are able to pass the test with flying colors. The Holy Spirit is similar to that.

He is the voice in your heart and head that helps, leads, and guides you. In the Bible, we find Him described as an advocate, a comforter, a counselor, and a helper. He leads us to the truth, teaches us right from wrong, reminds us of God's Word when we need it, and never leaves us. As I was writing this section, it became very clear to me that the Holy Spirit is the exact opposite of Satan's evil spirit in our lives. Take a look at these comparisons.

The Holy Spirit	**Satan's Spirit**
Desires to help you	Desires to "steal, kill, and destroy" you
Leads you closer to God and helps you make the right choices	Leads you away from God and tempts you with the wrong choices
Leads you to the right source for whatever you need	Uses your need to lead you into bondage through the wrong sources
Brings you true and lasting comfort	Desires to hurt and defeat you
Embraces you with God's love and holy presence	Tries to fill your life with the wrong people or influences
Is given only to God's people	Is present with everybody—including God's people
Loves you	Hates you
Helps transform your life for the better	Leads you deeper into sinfulness and self-destruction
Is always right and leads you to the truth	Is a liar and is always ultimately wrong—though he may cleverly twist the truth

You get the picture, right? The Holy Spirit is a phenomenal and gracious gift from God. Take another look at the table and understand how He helps us. Without Him, we have no power against our own sinful desires, negative outside influences, or Satan. With Him, we can have the blessed life that God desires for us. However, having the Holy Spirit is just a part of the equation. In order for Him to do God's work within us, we must listen to Him and follow His direction.

How do we hear Him?

Hearing the Holy Spirit's voice can be tricky. It can be particularly challenging if your head is filled with a lot of voices already. I'm not suggesting that you may have mental health challenges, only that some of us can still hear our parents' voices in our heads along with our own thoughts. Add Satan's voice to that mix and many others that our brains call to mind now and again. How do you sort them out and distinguish them from the Holy Spirit's voice?

In this book, I will share with you the importance of prayer and reading the Bible. They both help us hear the Holy Spirit. When we read the Bible, we learn to understand God's character. We become familiar with how He answers prayers. We learn about His likes and dislikes, and we get to know God. Just as a baby can recognize his mother's voice from all others, you will recognize your heavenly Father's voice. In the Bible scripture John 10:27, we read where Jesus said "My sheep hear My voice, and I know them, and they follow me." As we get to know God and tune our ears to His voice, we sharpen our ability to pick it out from the other voices clamoring for our attention.

The next great question is, When will you hear the Holy Spirit? You'll hear Him when He is doing His work. For example, you will hear Him when God responds to your prayers. If the answer requires an action from you, the Holy Spirit will tell you what to do. If God's response requires an action by someone else, the Holy Spirit will tell you to be patient and will encourage you to trust God. When you build the habit of praying all day and about everything, you can expect to hear the Spirit's voice all day.

Another time you'll hear Him will be when God is directing you. It may be as simple as Him telling you to go left instead of going right or to do or not do something. You'll also hear the Spirit when you need correction. He'll tell you that you shouldn't have said or done something. Then he'll push you to apologize to God and others and to make it right if you can.

The Holy Spirit speaks to us when we need encouragement or when we feel inadequate, sad, or even depressed. He reminds us of

God's love, His faithfulness, His acceptance, and His power. When we are afraid, the Holy Spirit calms our fears by reminding us that God is in control of everything at all times. When we feel lonely, the Holy Spirit reminds us that God will never leave or abandon us.

The Steroid Effect

There is another dynamic of the Holy Spirit that is also quite amazing. Through the Holy Spirit, God gives us access to a realm of capabilities that are undeniably beyond ourselves—let's call it the steroid effect. God has designed each of us to contribute to this world in a special way. His Spirit within us enhances our natural talents and abilities in ways that enable us to excel. We find ourselves to be more creative, stronger, faster, better at problem solving, more effective at our jobs, and better learners. He gives us access to God's power to have a positive impact on others and on this world. Unbelievers do not have this advantage. Satan offers them "advantages" that lead to his destructive and empty rewards.

As we begin to listen and follow the Holy Spirit, something starts happening. God begins to transform us, and we become more like Jesus Christ. We learn to trust God more, and it becomes easier to hear His voice and to follow His way. Our lives begin to change, and we mature as Christians. Gradually, we start producing good works (fruit) for God, and Satan and unbelievers have decreasingly less influence on us. Look at what the Bible tells us:

> But the Holy Spirit produces this kind of fruit in our lives: love, joy, peace, patience, kindness, goodness, faithfulness, gentleness, and self-control. There is no law against these things! (Galatians 5:22–23 NLT)

The Holy Spirit helps to transform us into who God wants us to be in this world. We are unable to achieve these character changes on our own. Through the Holy Spirit's work in us, we are able to achieve the freedom and abundant life that Jesus died for us to have.

The Holy Spirit guides, but you decide

I hope you understand now who the Holy Spirit is and that He is a part of God and is a wonderful gift from God. And it's obvious that following Him is the way to live. However, as Christians, there are times when we are tempted to do something that doesn't please God or when we just don't choose to listen to or trust His Spirit. This leads us to an extremely important point: in all cases, you have the choice of listening to and following the Holy Spirit or refusing and following your own way or Satan's. It's called free will. But understand that the Holy Spirit is always right. Choosing to disobey God is wrong (definition of a sin) and has its consequences, and we are not exempt from suffering consequences.

Fortunately, although God has given us the Holy Spirit, He knows that we will not achieve perfection in our human bodies. We will suffer consequences for making wrong choices, but He still covers us with His love, mercy, and grace. We should continually strive to follow God's way. It won't always be the easy way; it's usually never the popular way, and it often isn't the logical way (based on our limited knowledge), but it is *always* the right way.

The Holy Spirit is God's way of giving us what we need to be effective in this life and to prepare us for our life with Him. It is a privilege to have the Holy Spirit. We couldn't afford to pay Him if we were required to. We received Him for free, though we do not deserve it. Our God is wonderful.

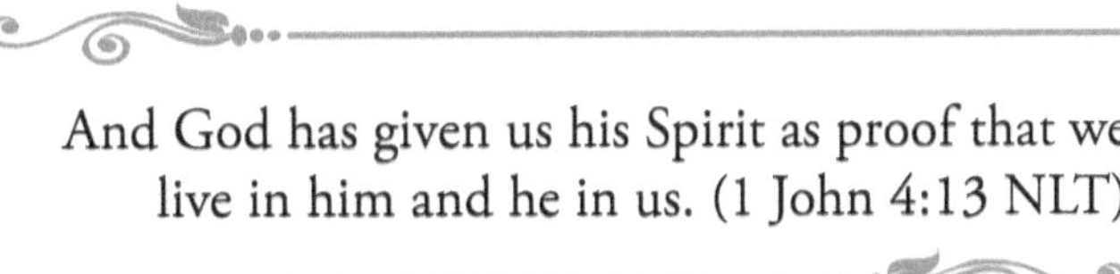

And God has given us his Spirit as proof that we live in him and he in us. (1 John 4:13 NLT)

Chapter 4

Talk to God Through Prayer

Pray without ceasing.

—1 Thessalonians 5:17

When my husband and I were dating, we spent many hours on the telephone every evening sharing stories about our lives, our day, and anything else that came up during the conversation. Even if we had seen each other that day, I looked forward to talking to him during the evening and missed him when we were apart. Those times were important in helping us get to know each other and helping to form the bond that we share today as husband and wife. I seriously doubt that we would have built a strong relationship if we never made time to talk.

Communication is an essential part of building and maintaining a close relationship with anyone, including God. We communicate with God and maintain a relationship with Him through prayer. Prayer is a way to spend focused time with God every day. Out of all of the people that you may talk with during a given day, your time talking with God is the most important and should not be missed, disregarded, or minimized.

How should we pray?

For whatever reason, the thought of praying can be intimidating for some people. Many wonder about the right way to pray. The good news is that praying is simply having a conversation with God. You don't need to use formal words—such as "Father, though knowest me" (unless that's your style). Just as you wouldn't feel the need to talk to a close friend using the language of William Shakespeare, you don't need to sound any particular way to talk to God. Some who are very skilled communicators may use well-crafted words and phrases when they pray, but God is just fine with plain language. He knows you, and He can hear your voice. He's not looking for you to impress Him with your words. He just wants you to speak to Him from your heart. It's more important to focus on *who* you are praying to and *what* you should pray for.

Who are we praying to?

When you are praying to God, it's important to understand that because of Jesus, you have the privilege of communicating directly with the most important and most powerful being in the universe. What's even more exciting is that He knows your name, and He wants to hear from you. Isn't that awesome? Let's look further into exactly who it is that we are communicating with.

In Jesus's model prayer, commonly known as the Lord's Prayer, He starts with the words "Our Father, which art in Heaven, Hallowed be thy name" (Matthew 6:9 KJV). By using the word *Father*, Jesus is telling us that God has a father-child relationship with us. When we pray, we are talking to our Father—someone who knows us, cares for us, has responsibility for us, and has power over our circumstances.

"Which art in Heaven" clarifies which father He is. God is not our earthly, biological father. He is the Father of all fathers and the ultimate head of all our lives.

In the last part of that sentence, we find that God's name is to be hallowed. The American Heritage Dictionary defines the verb *hallow* as "to make or set apart as holy; to respect or honor greatly."[2]

So when you pray, you are praying to your heavenly Father, and you are to do so with honor and great respect. Although we can speak to Him freely, openly, and honestly, we should always respect His authority, His power, and His wisdom.

You should also pray with faith that God is able to supply everything that you need. There is no situation that you will ever face in life that God is unable to handle. He has shown us His power through many Bible stories helping us to learn that there is nothing too hard for Him. He tells us in His Word that we should give Him our fears and troubles to handle because He cares for us (1 Peter 5:7). We do that through prayer. So when you pray, always be mindful that you are connecting with a caring heavenly Father who is fully able to meet your needs. He loves you and wants to hear from you.

What should we pray for?

Paul, the writer of much of the New Testament, answers this question well in Philippians 4:6 (NLT) where he writes, "Don't worry about anything; instead, pray about everything. Tell God what you need, and thank him for all He has done." *Everything* means every decision, need, desire, goal, question, concern, fear, hurt, issue—it means *all* things. God desires to help you in every area of your life every day of your life. Talk to Him about whatever is on your mind. Ask for His direction. He always knows what is best and *always* has your best interest at heart. He can see into the future, and He can control every outcome no matter how things appear to you.

Not only should you talk to God about your needs, but you should also pray for others. Your prayers should not always be about you. Ask God to bless and keep your loved ones each day. When you are aware of a need that someone has, take it to God. Oftentimes, we are unable to offer direct help to a person, but we can go to God on his or her behalf. This is called intercessory prayer. Because we have a connection with God, He hears us and will answer all our prayers.

We also must devote time in prayer toward thanking God for what He has done. Parents expect their children to ask for things, but they delight in being thanked for what has already been given.

Saying "thank you" tells the giver that you recognize and appreciate what he or she has done. It says that you realize that the giver made a conscious choice to do something good for you. As a new Christian, you may be able to call to mind only a few things to thank God for, and that's okay. The better you get to know Him, the more you'll see His works, and you'll have endless things to thank Him for.

When should we pray?

There is a scripture in the Bible that tells us to "never stop praying" (1 Thessalonians 5:17 NLT). This means that we are to pray all the time. The first time that I read it, I imagined people on the street and in the subway blocking pedestrians as they suddenly knelt and bowed their heads in prayer. That's not what it means. Though you should regularly have private moments of prayer, during which you kneel before God, more often, you will have mental moments of prayer. Mental moments happen throughout your day as you seek God's direction or give Him thanks.

Here are examples of how prayer can become a part of each day:

- When you wake up, thank God for a new day. Ask that He provide for and protect you and your family. Ask Him to guide you and give you wisdom and the courage to live a life that pleases Him.

- Pray over your meals, thanking God for providing and asking that He bless the food, bless the resources who provided it, and help the food to nourish your body.

- When you leave home, ask God to guide your travels and keep you safe.

- Pray for your church, community, neighbors, coworkers, managers, and friends. Pray for those who are ill or troubled.

- Pray that God will strengthen fellow believers. Pray that unbelievers will choose Jesus and be saved.

- When you read your Bible, ask God to give you understanding.

- Before you go to bed, thank God for protecting and keeping you and your family through the day. Ask for forgiveness for anything that you may have done that was not pleasing to Him. Ask Him to keep you and your loved ones safe through the night.

These are ways that you can make prayer a regular part of your day and life. The phrase "His telephone line is never busy" may be a cliché, but it's true. God is always there to listen to you. His availability is just one of the things that make Him the best friend you'll ever have.

Enhancing prayer through fasting

There are times during our lives as Christians when we go before God with a special need or request. God certainly hears all our prayers. But sometimes, we face a challenge or a need that is so great that we desire a heightened level of communication with Him. It is in these times that we fast—meaning "to abstain from specific foods or activities"—for a period time.

When we fast from something that we are accustomed to eating or doing daily, our bodies and minds will crave it. The physical craving serves as a reminder to us to pray. Interestingly, as we deny our bodies, our spiritual connection with God is strengthened, and our focus on Him is increased. Fasting is not a requirement; it is a choice that we make when we desire to gain a deeper connection with God.

How does God answer our prayers?

This book would be remiss if it addressed only one side of communicating with God without describing how He responds. First of all, He always responds either by His actions or by His voice. Second, although He may not answer when you want Him to, His answer comes when you need it and according to His timing. Third, He may not give you the answer that you wanted or expected. Last, His answer is always the right one and it comes at the right time—though often, you won't realize it until much later. Let's look at a few examples of prayers and God's responses.

Prayer:	**God's answer:**
"God please help me to pass this test." (You do your part by studying.)	He gives you understanding directly or through a helper. He may even lead your teacher to give you a break.
Prayer:	**God's answer:**
"God please help me buy this car *if* it is the best choice and best timing for me." (You do your part by preparing and selecting wisely.)	If you weren't able to get the car, His answer was no. If you received it months or years later, His answer was "not now." If you received it right away without forcing it to happen, His answer was yes.

Your role in every situation is to perform your part of the request responsibly and then to trust and follow Him.

But what if you don't like His answers? Your role in all cases is to trust and follow God. This can be difficult because, as humans, we often think that we know the right answer. Also, Satan capitalizes on our disappointment to make us question God's existence and love for us. He will present a different option (cheat on the test or steal a car) where we can divert from God's path to increase the chances of getting what we want. It is during these times that we must remain faithful. Always trust God and follow Him.

As you grow in your relationship with God, over time, you will understand how He works, and you'll have living proof of His loving hand in your life. It will take you longer to learn this lesson if you leave God's road in favor of Satan's to get your way.

What if we've prayed and God didn't answer?

If you already have experience with prayer, you may feel that some of your most desperate prayers went unanswered. You may also think that God did not hear your prayer because the worst possible outcome happened. Perhaps you felt abandoned by God. Your disappointment may have caused you to no longer believe in the power of prayer. Always know that God hears and is in control.

If you prayed before you accepted Jesus, understand that you were not praying to your Father. You were addressing someone that you didn't have a relationship with who had no obligation to hear and respond to you. This may seem harsh, but God responds to those who believe in Him—His children. He does not want to be used for human convenience.

Yet even Christians have had prayers that we felt went unanswered. This is largely because we didn't get the answer that we expected and because, as humans, we are incapable of seeing the big picture. In all instances, however, God answers; and in all cases, we eventually see the wisdom of His response.

Many times, the problem is that we want God to carry out our plans instead of asking Him to work His plan through our lives. We think we know what is best for ourselves and for others. Believe me, we don't. We also tend to think that God's answers should always lead to our immediate comfort and joy. Not so. In these lives, we will experience difficult seasons, but God will help us through them all (Psalms 34:19).

Three things to avoid when praying

Be aware that Satan desires to occupy every area of your life—including your prayer time. Remember, Satan desires to kill, steal, and destroy everything good in your life (John 10:10). He'll try to intercept something as precious as prayer to entice the human parts of us to make it a selfish act. Here are three important things that you should avoid:

1. *Don't pray to impress other people (Matthew 6:5,7).* Although you may be good with words, the goal of prayer should never be to receive accolades from others. It should always be to communicate sincerely with God.

2. *Don't pray only when you want something.* God will supply all of your needs (Philippians 4:19), and he is able to bless you beyond anything that you can imagine (Ephesians 3:20). Ask God to fulfill His plan for your life, then trust Him. Don't build your prayer life solely around requests that you want to be fulfilled.

3. *Don't forget to pray.* When you forget to pray or don't make time for it, you're attempting to handle life on your own. God is infinitely smarter than us. We all need Him. Therefore, we all need to pray.

Above all else, be sincere when you pray. Don't make it a thoughtless habit, and don't doubt God or His power. Know that you're praying to a God who hears and is able to respond with the correct and timely answer. Pray regularly and about everything. Pray for others and for yourself. Thank God for what He has done. Trust His answers.

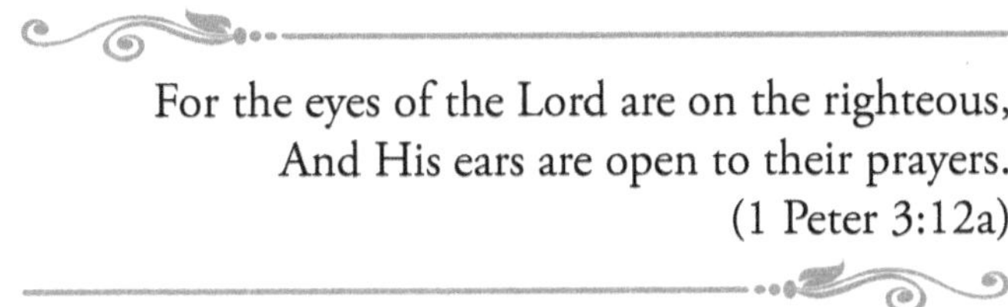

> For the eyes of the Lord are on the righteous,
> And His ears are open to their prayers.
> (1 Peter 3:12a)

Thoughts, Reflections, and Questions

Chapter 5

Read the Bible—God's Word

Your word is a lamp to my feet and a light to my path.
—Psalms 119:105

The most important of all the books ever written and the best-selling one of all time is the Holy Bible. In it, we learn about God the Father and how we can live to please Him, His Son Jesus Christ, the Holy Spirit, the mysteries of life and death, the beginning of times, and the end of times. It is the only book that can and should be used to guide your entire life. The Bible is an important gift from God and is an essential part of getting to know Him.

What is the Bible?

The word *bible* means book of books, and that's exactly what it is. The protestant Bible is a collection of sixty-six books.[3] The first thirty-nine are grouped as the Old Testament. The remaining twenty-seven comprise the New Testament. God inspired at least forty authors to write the books of the Bible over the span of 1,500 years. It has been originally written in Hebrew, Aramaic, and Greek and has since been translated to more than 2,018 languages (and counting!).[4]

The Old Testament records historical information from the creation of the earth through about four hundred years before the coming of Jesus Christ. In it, we learn about Adam and Eve, the birth of the nation of Israel (God's chosen people), God's laws, and a host of miracles and stories of deliverance. We also read beautiful love stories and others of lust, scandal, and war. In it, we find poetry, songs, and receive timeless words of wisdom. We gain insight into how obedience can lead to God's blessings and how disobedience can lead to His wrath.

The New Testament chronicles the human birth, life, death, and the resurrection of Jesus Christ. Through writers who walked beside Him, we learn of His power through the miracles that he performed and His love for us through His death on the cross. The New Testament shares the birth of the Christian church and the persecution of early followers. It imparts to us principles for every aspect of Christian living. The Bible ends with the book of Revelation in which God gives us a preview of the end times.

The Bible covers life on earth from its creation to its end and gives examples and instruction on everything in between. It provides us direction on how to live our lives from the beginning of our lives on earth until our deaths.

Why should we read it?

Spending personal time reading the Word of God is critical for every Christian. Reading God's Word helps us to know the truth about Him, ourselves, and Satan. It is the spiritual food that nourishes us and helps us to mature as Christians. Consider this verse:

> All Scripture is inspired by God and is useful
> to teach us what is true and to make us realize
> what is wrong in our lives. It corrects us when
> we are wrong and teaches us to do what is right.
> God uses it to prepare and equip his people to
> do every good work. (2 Timothy 3:16–17 NLT)

Unfortunately, there are far too many Christians who do not read the Bible regularly or at all. They claim to believe what it says, but they are too busy, don't like to read, don't understand it, or just don't have the desire to read it. This is great news for Satan. He knows that the Christian who does not read the Word of God has little power to use against him. He can tell them all sorts of lies, and because they aren't knowledgeable in what God says, they will fall for the lies or exist in a continuous state of uncertainty or confusion. As a new Christian, you can't afford to fall victim to this. Decide today that you will make the time to read the Bible every day.

How to get started

There are two common approaches to building a daily Bible reading habit. One approach is to read various Bible passages daily using devotionals. You can subscribe to a daily devotional, such as *Our Daily Bread*,[5] or *Today in the Word*.[6] You can also download a Bible app, such as YouVersion[7], which has a large library of wonderful reading plans. Devotionals and reading plans typically give you short Bible passages to read each day and include an explanation of the readings. The writers help you understand the scriptures, and the daily schedule helps you to build the habit of reading.

If you'd like to jump right into reading the Bible, you can find devotionals that will guide you through the entire Bible. You should also purchase a physical study Bible. Three major Bible publishers—Tyndale House, Thomas Nelson, and Zondervan—have excellent study Bibles with notes that help explain the scriptures. Although the gift Bibles, such as the Gideon Bibles, often available in hotel rooms and in church pews are inexpensive, most people can use a little help understanding what they are reading. Study Bibles provide many tools to help clarify scriptures, highlight themes, define unusual terms, and help the reader obtain an overall understanding of the text.

When shopping for a Bible, take time to read a few verses before you make a purchase. It is very important that you are able to comprehend what you read. The most well-known and quoted Bible translation is the King James Version (KJV). But though the older English language is beautiful, it can be difficult for a new reader (and even an experienced one at times) to understand.

Newer translations are available in more modern English. The New King James Version (NKJV), the New Living Translation (NLT), and the New International Version (NIV) are examples of these updated translations. Some people have a strong preference for the King James Version and feel that it is the only one that should be read. But God never decreed that. He wants you to read and understand His Word in a form that you can understand.

After buying your Bible, read the information in the front of the book to understand the layout and how to use the tools (e.g., notes, references, tables, and maps). Establish a daily reading goal, such as reading one chapter a day. You can begin with Genesis and read through Revelation, or you can start with the book of Psalms or Proverbs. Perhaps you'd like to start with the New Testament book of Matthew or James. The important thing is to start somewhere. Ask God to speak to your heart and help you receive His intended message from what you read each day. The Holy Spirit will help you understand, and you'll find yourself growing, learning, and gaining wisdom and insight through God's Word.

Plan to read the whole Bible

An amazing number of people have read a popular series of fictional novels that have a combined total of more than 4,100 (US) pages. Children and adults across the globe have waited in long lines to purchase the books, and some were unable to sleep until they finished reading the latest installment.

The Bible on my nightstand has fewer than 2,200 pages. Without the commentaries and tables, it would be even shorter. Satan tells people that the Bible is boring, outdated, too long, scary, impossible, and even unnecessary to read. But he is a liar and deceiver. He knows that if you read it, you'll know the truth, and the truth will set you free. You'll be stronger, wiser, and well-equipped to live a life that pleases God. No matter how long it takes you—two years, five years, or ten years—you should read all sixty-six books. God has something in every one of them just for you.

Is the Old Testament still relevant?

Some say that it is only necessary to read the New Testament because the Old Testament is no longer relevant. Don't believe it. That is one of Satan's attempts to limit your knowledge. If you picked up a novel and started reading it from the middle, you'd miss critical information that would help you understand the full story. The same is true for the Bible. The Old Testament is just as relevant and important as the New Testament. In it, we find answers, help, strength, and a tremendous amount of wisdom. There are amazing stories that give us an in-depth view of God's character and capabilities.

The Old Testament also helps us to better understand the New Testament. There are ceremonial and civil laws in the Old Testament that we are no longer required to follow because of Jesus Christ. But it is still important to know them because they give us a greater appreciation for the sacrifice that Jesus Christ made for us and for God's mercy and grace.

What if you need help understanding?

If you find that as you get started, you need help understanding the scriptures, pray and ask God to give you an understanding and to send someone to help you. You cannot listen to everybody's explanation of the scriptures (Satan will offer to help you). Your church pastor, ministers, or Bible teachers should be good sources for help. You can also learn by attending a church Bible class. You may even have a family member or friend who can explain a scripture for you. Even if you don't understand everything, keep reading. You'll get more comfortable with the language and style as you go. Often, the message gets clearer as you read on.

How can you be sure that the Bible is true?

This is an important question because the entire Christian faith is hinged on believing that everything that we read in the Bible is true. There has never been a time when the scriptures have not been questioned. Many have concluded that the Bible does not represent truth. Others have changed portions of the Bible to reflect what they can believe. So how can we have any degree of certainty that the Bible is true?

Consider this: The Bible includes scriptures that tell us about the past, teach us how to live for God in the present, and tell us what will happen in the future. Of course, we cannot know for certain what happened in the ancient past because we were not there. Nor can we know the future because it has not yet arrived. But in our own lifetimes, we can see that God's promises to us are true. When we read the Bible, get to know God personally, and experience His work in our lives, we witness the truth of His Word in the present day.

Bible verse, Hebrews 13:8, reads, "Jesus Christ is the same yesterday, today, and forever." As we feel His presence, see His miracles, receive His love, grace, mercy, forgiveness, protection, and peace in our lives today, we find that He is who He says He is. The Holy Spirit helps us to learn through our experiences that God can do what He says He will do. Based on this, we have no doubt that the stories of the past are true. And we are able to completely trust that His prophecies of the future will come to pass.

There is another unexplainable reason that we can trust the Bible—the soul knows the truth. God's Word nourishes the soul. When we read the Bible, it's like drinking a cool glass of water on a hot day. Our spirits are strengthened and fed in a way that no other source can accomplish. As humans, we cannot properly explain it because we have limited understanding. But Christians know what we feel.

Put your faith in God and believe His Word. God gave us the Bible to teach us, direct us, correct us, guide our paths, and nourish our souls. You'll be pleasantly surprised at how interesting and exciting many of the Bible stories are and how God will use His Word to transform your life. You cannot truly know God without reading and regularly feasting on His Word.

The Word of the Lord is proven. He is a shield to all who trust in Him. (2 Samuel 22:31b)

Thoughts, Reflections, and Questions

Chapter 6

Make Time to Meditate and Reflect

Many, O Lord my God, are Your wonderful
works which You have done.

—Psalms 40:5

Sometimes when you read the Bible, attend Bible Class, and hear the Word at church services, you may feel as though you've taken in a lot of information. If it were food for the physical body, your mouth might be quite full. Imagine yourself sitting home on a Sunday afternoon with protruding jaws after having eaten a great meal. If you keep the food in your mouth, it will not do the rest of your body much good.

Like food, we have to digest God's Word. We do this by making time to think about and reflect on what we've heard so that it can become a part of us. There are many people who never digest the Word, and as a result, mature very slowly—if they ever do.

Make time in your day to meditate on what God has told you through His Word. What did God tell you about who He is—His power, knowledge, presence? What did He tell you about His love for you and His ability to meet your needs? What did He tell you about what you are able to achieve through Him? Did it give you more strength? Did it give you more courage? Did it give you more joy? Think about it.

Reflection involves making time to see God's work. I have heard people say that they are unable to see God, so it's hard for them to believe. Christians can experience that feeling also if they don't make time for reflection. One way that we can see God is by looking at the beautiful, creative, and highly advanced things that He created—humans, bugs, whales, stars, trees, waterfalls—the list is amazing. You can also see Him through things that others have created with gifts that He gave them such as beautiful art, music, sculptures, skyscrapers, and airplanes. Start viewing things as God's wonderful creations and know that "whatever is good and perfect is a gift coming down to us from God our Father, who created all the lights in the heavens" (James 1:17 NLT).

Also remember the wonderful things that God has done in your life. Think about the many ways that He has blessed you by meeting your needs, solving your problems, and regulating your mind. Think about the miracles that God performed in your life—the peace miracles, financial miracles, love miracles, and medical miracles. Make time to recall and appreciate the works of His hands.

How do Christians meditate and reflect?

Many of us are familiar with meditation techniques practiced by other religious groups such as Buddhism. Christians don't have a prescribed method that involves a particular posture, chant, or other action. For us, it is as simple as tuning out all other noise to enjoy quiet time with God.

Some Christians meditate and reflect after reading their Bibles. They read a passage of scripture, ponder what it means, then think about how God has confirmed the scripture through His actions in their lives. Others have busy schedules and can rarely slow down long enough to sit and think quietly for long periods of time, so we multi-task. We meditate and reflect while completing our chores, exercising, or engaging in some other activity that allows us to mentally escape.

In addition to our quiet times, there are other activities that help Christians focus their thoughts on the Word and works of God. The first is scripture memorization. As you read the Bible, you will find scriptures that seem to leap from the page and speak directly to your heart. For example, a common scripture that many people have memorized is John 3:16, "For God so loved the world that He gave His only begotten Son, that whoever believes in Him should not perish but have everlasting life." We memorize this verse because it brings us joy and gives us insight into God's love for us. Once memorized, the Holy Spirit helps us recall it whenever we want without having a Bible in hand.

Christian music is another resource that helps us to meditate and reflect. The lyrics of Christian songs are often taken directly from the scriptures. The lyrics may be expressions of worship and thanksgiving, reflections on things that God has done, reminders of what God can do, prayers, songs of hope, or a combination.

Like secular music, Christian music can have a mood-altering affect. If you are happy, a joyful song can focus your gratitude on God and keep your spirit high. If you are worried, lonely, or sad, a song that reminds you of God's love, care, and power can bring you comfort. Christian songs can be found in practically all music styles—pop, rock, country, traditional gospel, opera, jazz, and even hip-hop. You're sure to find many favorites in the styles of your choice.

Journaling can also facilitate mediation and reflection. As you read the Bible, when you come across passages that resonate with you, you can write about them in your journal. You can record what the scriptures mean to you and how they help you. Some Christians also write about their current challenges or experiences and write their prayers to God. These types of entries are interesting to review periodically. They become personal reminders of how God has answered your prayers and has used His power to meet your needs.

Christians also reflect through sharing with others. When speaking with a family member or friend, we can share something that we read in the Bible, our current memory verse, new insights, a blessing, or experience with God. Sharing helps us to reflect and witness to others.

The amazing benefits

Unlike praying, reading the Bible, and listening to the Holy Spirit, this activity may seem to be less important, maybe even optional. But it isn't. It's during our quiet times with God that the Holy Spirit helps us to connect God's Word with our lives. For example, God has told us in His Word that He will supply all our needs (Philippians 4:19). When we meditate on that scripture and then think about the state of our lives, we realize that it is true. There may be a shiny new object that we would like to have, but we recognize that God has provided everything that we truly need.

As we meditate on the scriptures and find repeatedly that God is true to His Word, our faith and strength increase. Remembering what God has done for us helps us when we face the next challenge. As a result, we begin to trust God more and worry less. Less worry leads to lesser stress, better health, and greater peace. We can trust that if God has brought us through our difficult situations in the past, He is very aware of what is happening in our lives and is able to deliver us again.

Through meditation and reflection, we increasingly understand that God the Creator is also God our Father, protector and provider. We build a personal relationship and learn to depend completely on Him.

As we begin to acknowledge God's hand in our lives, something interesting happens: we find ourselves praising and worshipping Him at every opportunity. We praise God for what He has done—showered us with His love, goodness, and mercy. We worship Him for who He is—our all-powerful, all-knowing, ever-present help. We become deeply grateful for all He has done in our lives. When we reach that place in our knowledge and appreciation of God, we trust Him more and become more committed to living for Him.

That's our ultimate goal here on earth: to live our lives in a way that pleases God and reflects His character. Take time regularly to meditate on and digest God's Word and to reflect on His wondrous works in your life. Realize for yourself that God's Word has proven true for you.

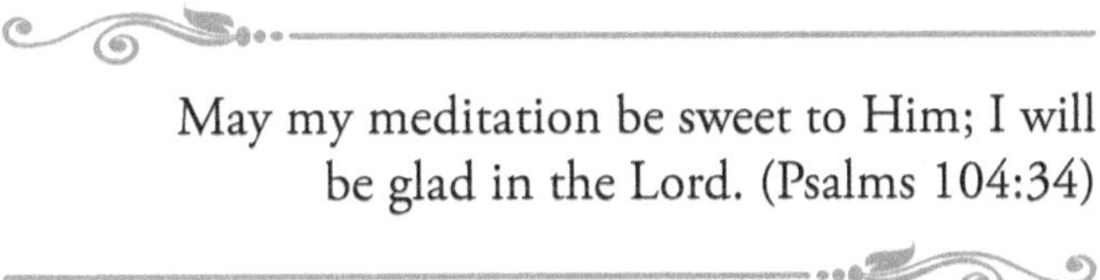

May my meditation be sweet to Him; I will
be glad in the Lord. (Psalms 104:34)

Thoughts, Reflections, and Questions

Chapter 7

Join a Church Family

And let us not neglect our meeting together, as some
people do, but encourage one another, especially
now that the day of his return is near.

—Hebrews 10:25

Everything that I've encouraged you to do so far—pray, read the Bible, listen to the Holy Spirit, meditate, and reflect—are things that you can do alone and from the comfort of your home. All of those actions help to build your personal relationship with God. Although we can do many things alone, we are also created to be in relationships with and to work with others. You are a part of the body of Christ. Therefore, you need to connect with the rest of the body—God's church.

Take a look at your leg. By itself, it's probably a great leg. It may be muscular and well-toned (it's okay if it isn't). But it can't fully achieve its purpose all alone. It needs the hip, thigh, ankle, and foot. It needs veins, arteries, capillaries, blood, and everything else. But even that's not enough. The leg also needs help to perform its responsibilities. In this case, another leg would be extremely helpful. God designed all of our human body parts to work together so that we can operate effectively.

The same is true of God's church. All who have accepted Jesus as their Savior together are His church. Because we cannot all gather together in one place on a regular basis as was possible for the early believers, we branch off into church families. You are a part of a church family. If you haven't found one yet, it's missing you. Ask God to lead you to the place of worship that is in His plan for you. Then visit different churches until you feel in your heart that God has led you to join one.

Why is joining a church necessary?

The Bible tells us:

> And let us not neglect our meeting together, as some people do, but encourage one another, especially now that the day of his return is drawing near. (Hebrews 10:20 NLT)

Just as all of the other instructions from God have a positive purpose for our lives, so does attending church. One important purpose for attending church is to grow spiritually. Consider these verses:

> Now these are the gifts Christ gave to the church: the apostles, the prophets, the evangelists, and the pastors and teachers. Their responsibility is to equip God's people to do his work and build up the church, the body of Christ. This will continue until we all come to such unity in our faith and knowledge of God's Son that we will be mature in the Lord, measuring up to the full and complete standard of Christ. (Ephesians 4:11–13 NLT)

God has given His people special responsibilities and gifts to help you understand the Bible, get to know Him better, serve others, and to mature as a Christian. It isn't very likely that these people will show up at your home regularly to give you personalized training and support for the rest of your life. And although televised church services may be convenient, unless you are bedridden or are unable to leave your home, they should serve only as a supplement to regular church attendance. You wouldn't expect a child to function well in society by only watching educational television shows. Likewise, you can't expect to reach Christian maturity by doing so either.

When you attend a Christ-focused church, you will hear the Word of God explained in sermons and in Bible classes. There will be people there who are responsible for helping you understand God's Word and can answer your questions. They can give you special counsel and help you apply God's Word and principles to your life. They can share faith-building testimonies of God's work in their lives.

In addition to learning in church, you also have the opportunity to develop relationships with other Christians. There are people who are walking with the Lord faithfully and are full of love, peace, and joy. They are standing ready to love everyone who comes near them. It's awesome. I experience this every week. God has equipped His churches to help meet the needs of His people. In His church, the members encourage and strengthen one another. They help out when someone is in need. They become the body of Jesus Christ, seeing others through God's eyes and using all their abilities to do His work.

This does not mean that everyone in church will reflect God's character at all times. You can't expect that at any church. No one is perfect, nor will we ever be. Even those who we hold in high regard make mistakes. Even those whom we have seen live righteous lives will err. Also, there are members of the church family who are still in the early stages of their Christian growth.

The key is that we acknowledge our missteps (not excuse them), repent (apologize to God and make better choices), and consciously try to live lives that please God every day. True Christians are sorry when they do wrong. The Holy Spirit helps to correct and redirect us. The body of Christ helps to build us back up.

Be aware that not everyone who attends church is truly seeking to please God or mature in Christ. Some attend out of religious habit. They have no desire to grow, learn, or live as God commanded. They may not even believe in God. Know also that Satan has planted people in church. They seek to cause trouble, cast doubts, and prevent the message and works of Christ from succeeding. They are not there to love, encourage, or strengthen you.

When you hear others say "Christians are worse than everybody else," they include those who attend church and profess to be Christians yet live in a manner that gives Christ and His followers a bad name. But don't worry or let them keep you away. In God's church, His people are well-equipped and effective in carrying out His purposes. Our hope is that God will touch their hearts and transform their lives.

What type of church should I join?

You probably noticed that there are a lot of churches. If you haven't found one already, it may be challenging to figure out which one to join. I'll offer you five things to look for when selecting your new church. The first is that it is a Christian church. This means that the church was founded on and operates under the belief that Jesus Christ is the Son of God, that He died on the cross and rose again, and that He has gone to prepare a place for His chosen people where they will be resurrected to eternal life with Him.

Many churches have posted, printed, or occasionally recited a version of the Apostles Creed. Below is the Old Roman version:

> I believe in God almighty
> And in Christ Jesus, his only Son, our Lord
> Who was born of the Holy Spirit and the Virgin
> Mary
> Who was crucified under Pontius Pilate and was
> buried
> And the third day rose from the dead
> Who ascended into heaven
> And sitteth on the right hand of the Father
> Whence he cometh to judge the living and the
> dead.
> And in the Holy Spirit
> The holy church
> The remission of sins
> The resurrection of the flesh
> The life everlasting.[8]

This is important because there are many churches that refer to their beliefs as Christian who do not believe this in its entirety—which means that they do not believe the entire Bible. If a church does not believe the entire Holy Bible, it is not the one that you should choose.

The second criterion is that the church's services are God-focused. In many churches today, the people have become worshippers of the priest, pastor, choir, or other church leader. These individuals or groups become the focus of worship and reason that the people attend. The members are trained to please him or her. They seek that person's favor and attention and, ultimately, hold the person in higher regard than God. This is a problem and is not where you should be. God is our strength and our source, and only He deserves our worship. This doesn't mean that a church leader cannot be respected and appreciated for his or her work for the Lord. But that person should not seek a higher position in the members' lives and hearts than God.

The third criterion is that the Holy Bible should be the primary source of information for the church. In addition to this, the members should be encouraged to read the Bible and develop a personal relationship with God. There are many churches today that consider other writings that are based on human wisdom to have equal importance with the Bible. If there is a conflict between the Bible and other writings, the Bible may be considered as less accurate. This is a problem. If a church rarely refers to Bible scripture, it may not be seeking to be a part of the body of Christ. God's people need His Word to live.

The fourth criterion is that the church has a passion for strengthening God's people, serving others and reaching those who do not know Christ. The church family should use its resources, abilities, and skills to make a positive impact in this world—not just to entertain and support one another. It is wonderful to worship and serve with people that you know and love, but God's church must also focus on obeying His commands. He has given His people the following mandate:

> Go therefore and make disciples of all the nations, baptizing them in the name of the Father and of the Son and of the Holy Spirit, teaching them to observe all things that I have commanded you. (Matthew 28:19–20a)

The fifth criterion is more subjective than the others. You must receive confirmation in your heart that God has led you to join a particular church family. So as you visit churches, look for evidence that the people are believers of the resurrected Christ, that God is the focus of the church, that the Bible is the church's authoritative source of information, that the church is on a mission to attract unbelievers to Christ by showing and sharing God's love, and that you feel God's confirmation in your heart that He wants you to join the church that you have selected.

How do I join a church?

Once you feel that you have found the church to which you desire to belong, the mechanics of joining the physical church are typically simple. In many cases, an invitation is given during the church service, where you join by getting up and walking to people or seats offered in the front. Some churches have other methods that are not as obvious.

If you're not sure when or how to become a part of a church, ask a greeter or someone who appears to already be a member. He or she should be quite happy to give you directions. That's the easy part. But simply stating that you would like to be a member does not automatically make you a part of the church family.

When you join a church, often the members are eager to have you become part of a group. But you may not be ready at that time. Truthfully, you probably need to continue growing spiritually and listening to God for direction. In fact, you should be doing both of those things. However, there are a few ways that you can become a functioning member of the church right away. These are the basics for Christians at all levels of spiritual maturity:

- *Attend regularly.* Begin building the habit of going to church regularly to hear God's Word. Attend church services and Bible classes to continuously gain knowledge and increase your understanding.

- *Get to know people.* As stated before, there are some exceptional people in church. God has added a new set of brothers and sisters to your life who will help support, encourage, and strengthen you.

- *Contribute financially.* Just like all other buildings, churches have utility bills, salaries to pay, and other financial obligations. They also need money to carry out the church's ministries. The money comes from members who contribute to the church as their way of giving a portion of what God has given them. If you don't have an income and are unable to give money, ask God to show you other ways that you can give (e.g., by donating time, talent, or items for those in need). He knows your heart and will still bless you and show you a way to support the church. It is a blessing to be able to give, and it is a requirement with a promise. The truth of this scripture has been confirmed time and again for Christians who give to the church freely:

  > Give, and you will receive. Your gift will return to you in full—pressed down, shaken together to make room for more, running over, and poured into your lap. The amount you give will determine the amount you get back. (Luke 6:38 NLT)

- *Pray for your church family.* All churches have struggles because Satan does not want them to be successful. Pray for God's people everywhere, that we can be strong and effective in living for Christ and drawing others to Him.

God will lead you to other ways in which you can take part in your church's ministries when the time is right.

What church is and isn't

Church should only be a *part* of your relationship with Christ; it should not solely define it. In other words, being a Christian is a lifestyle decision that goes far beyond the church doors. Your relationship with God should be nurtured every day.

For too many people, attending church is the extent of their relationship with Him. They practice church very well. They wear the right clothes, say the right things, do the right things, and know the right people—but all too often, they don't know God. They leave church with no power to live as God desires and no ability to share His love with others or to draw people to Him.

Church should be thought of as a charging station, where Christians are God's satellites. We are stationed throughout this world to make a positive impact on those around us. Individually, God teaches and empowers us to serve Him and live for Him. He also positions us (through His church families) to strengthen and recharge one another, to accomplish larger tasks together, and to receive and prepare new satellites for His service. Then we are sent back into the world to make a difference. Thus, our real work is outside of the church. And because of this, we have to be just as connected to God throughout the week as we are during our services.

Being an active member of a church family is necessary to grow, to serve, and to have the abundant life that God wants for you.

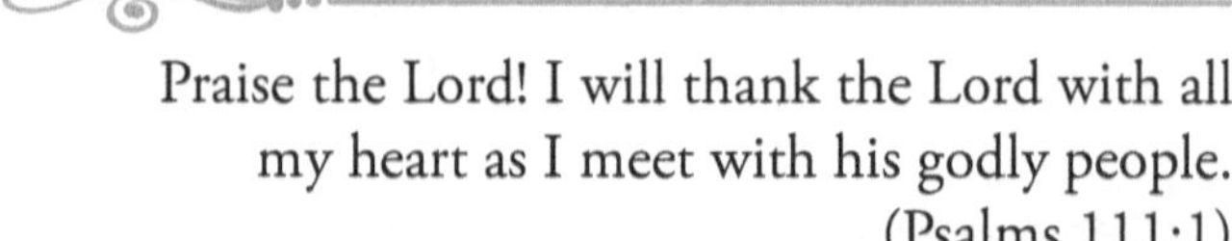

Praise the Lord! I will thank the Lord with all
my heart as I meet with his godly people.
(Psalms 111:1)

Thoughts, Reflections, and Questions

Chapter 8

Set New Priorities for Your Life

But seek first the kingdom of God and His righteousness,
and all these things shall be added to you.
—Matthew 6:33

When we really stop and think about it, it could probably be said that most of us live for ourselves. We make choices and take actions every day to achieve our goals. For example, I get up and go to work Monday through Friday to earn money, contribute positively to society, and make productive use of my time. I expect to use the money to help meet the needs of my family, to donate, and to enhance my life through entertainment and travel.

There are many people who share similar goals. When we live for ourselves, we believe that we will receive satisfaction in life when the goals we sought after are accomplished. But we always seem to crave more money, bigger houses, fancier cars, better clothes, more exotic travels, bigger televisions, faster computers, and so on and so forth. Before we know it, we're in debt up to our eyeballs, and we find that we have to work hard to maintain a lifestyle that never satisfies. We wake up one day and realize that we are in bondage. We find that we have to earn a certain income, maintain some relationship, or achieve a particular status to keep everything that we worked so hard for.

Satan knows that when living this life becomes our priority, we are ripe for picking. He loves our chase for the American Dream. As long as we are focused on pleasing ourselves, we can't be focused on pleasing God. And if we're not focused on pleasing God, by default, we'll be pleasing Satan. This is why, as Christians, we have to set new priorities for our lives. Am I suggesting that it is wrong to work hard to have nice things? Of course not. Nice things have a place in life, but we have to be very careful, else they will become gods in our lives.

Identify the gods in your life

Everyone, even the atheist, has consciously or unconsciously chosen one or more gods for their lives. It's part of being human. As Christians, before we accepted Christ as our Savior, there was someone or something that we felt was our source. For example, a great number of people idolize money. Everything that they do is motivated by their desire to obtain it.

It's true that money is the medium of exchange for items that we need. But it's a problem when we feel that we're worthless without it and begin to define ourselves and others by the amounts accumulated. And when we find ourselves doing whatever is necessary to have more and more of it, money becomes a god in our lives. Consider this news report from WLBT news in Atlanta:

> Suicide rates in the U.S. tend to rise and fall with the economy, according to a new report. CDC [Centers for Disease Control] researchers found the largest increase in suicides came during the Great Depression, while the lowest rates were during times of economic growth, like World War II and the Dot-com era. The risk was strongest among adults age 25 to 64, likely people who needed work.[9]

We've heard stories of wealthy people who committed suicide after sustaining a significant financial loss in the stock market. In many cases, they would have still been financially rich by normal standards. Why would more people commit suicide during an economic downturn? They do it because they don't know how they can make it without their god—money. And without possessing a certain amount of money, they feel hopeless.

This reality gives us the perfect formula for identifying the gods in our lives. Here's a brief exercise to help you determine the priorities in your life. Record everything and everyone that you feel that you *must have* and write them on the lines below. Anything is allowed except the very basic survival needs such as air, water, and reasonable amounts of food and clothing. Examples are money, sex, excitement, alcohol, mom, a job, and grandma. If you need to, close the book and take time to think about it. Be honest with yourself. This is between you and God only.

I know that I cannot live without

____

____

____

Now, take a look at the people or things that you listed. They may be very important to you and fulfill important needs in your life. For example, designer clothes may help you maintain a strong sense of self-esteem and a beloved parent may give you unconditional love and acceptance. Alcohol may calm your nerves or give you confidence and courage.

People and things can gradually become gods in our lives if we let them become our controlling forces, the sources of our strength, and our highest priorities. We can begin to rely on them to the extent that we honestly do not believe that we can live without them. Attachments to this degree can be mentally, spiritually, and physically unhealthy. They can also be unfair to people who didn't ask for that much responsibility in our lives. God will be everything that you need if you let Him. He provides unconditional love, comfort, peace, joy, food, strength—you name it. He offers, and He delivers.

Satan will gladly help us to erect gods in our lives and will tempt us to live with misplaced priorities to keep our focus completely off the true and living God. He knows that we are limited in our power and need something outside of ourselves to help us navigate life successfully. He'll suggest things to us, hoping that we will take the bait, become victim to bondage, live without a purpose, and ultimately destroy our lives. We can see how successful Satan has been by observing the lives of the careless rich and famous in the media. They appear to have attained everything yet have acquired nothing meaningful. Each of us is at risk of falling into that trap. But thank God for a better way.

Make pleasing God your priority

Consider Jesus's words as recorded in this scripture:

> Seek the Kingdom of God above all else, and live
> righteously, and He will give you everything you
> need. (Matthew 6:33 NLT)

What does it mean to "seek the kingdom of God"? It means that we strive to live under God's leadership while here on earth and that our ultimate goal is to spend eternity with Him in heaven. We seek Him by praying, studying His Word, listening to His voice, following His guidance, and striving to have a close and personal relationship with Him. Our desire is not to achieve praise and admiration from humans but to fulfill God's plan for our lives and to please Him. When we make pleasing God our priority, He will give us everything that we need. There are no limits.

Satan knows that people and things will fail us; they are not God, and they cannot help it. He also knows that when they fail us, we will seek a substitute—typically one that is self-destructive. But God never fails us. When He blesses and provides for us, His methods will lead to peace and joy. Here is scripture that affirms God's goodness: "The blessings of the Lord makes a person rich, and He adds no sorrow with it" (Proverbs 10:22 NLT). Our God can make us rich in ways that don't require us to sell our souls and through blessings that money can't buy and thieves can't steal.

God's children don't have to chase after what others consider to be important in this world. And those who don't share our desire to please God find us strange. They don't understand our choices and mindsets. We're thought of as different or peculiar. These differences cause them to avoid and often reject us. That is okay. Living to please God comes with worthwhile sacrifices. Sacrificing is rarely easy. Yet know that God will ensure that we have everyone and everything that we need to have blessed and satisfying lives.

You will never regret that you chose to live the life of a Christian because God makes life worth living. Without Him, the priorities that we choose and the goals that we achieve can leave us empty. Satan is constantly working to put other gods and priorities in our lives, but we must reject them all. There is no god but God. Make living for Him the focus and priority of your life.

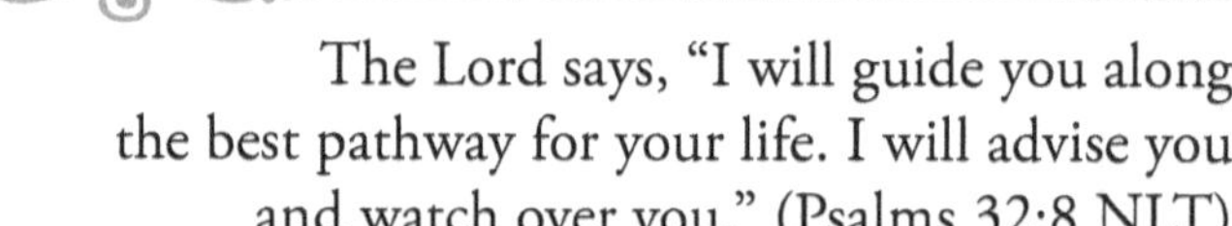

The Lord says, "I will guide you along the best pathway for your life. I will advise you and watch over you." (Psalms 32:8 NLT)

Thoughts, Reflections, and Questions

Chapter 9

Arm Yourself for Battle Each Day

We are human, but we don't wage war as humans do.
—2 Corinthians 10:3 NLT

Being a Christian and living the life of a believer is magnificent and deeply satisfying in many ways, but being a Christian is not easy. Although God is delighted to have you join His family, the angels are rejoicing over your decision, and millions of believers everywhere welcome you, Satan is not happy with you. When Satan is unhappy, he pitches a fit and becomes determined to get his way. Unbeknownst to you, when you became a Christian, you were placed on Satan's hit list for the rest of your life.

He'll be working continuously to get you to change your mind ("It's not worth it"), become discouraged ("I can't do this"), to not commit to it ("I'll get to it later"), or to just become too preoccupied and forget God altogether. You can count on Satan to work against everything that you have read thus far. Here's what you can expect from him:

When you	**Expect Satan to**
plan or start to pray and read the Bible	• tell you that you're too tired, • distract you during your prayer, • make you forget to do it, • get you to doubt its importance, • get you to doubt its truth, • tell you it's too hard, or • suggest that you do it later.
begin to meditate, reflect, and listen to the Holy Sprit	• give you a spirit of doubt or confusion; • attribute God's works to luck, coincidence, or human power; or • bind you with a spirit of fear.
find a church home	• get you to join a church that is not in God's plan for you, • tell you that church attendance is unnecessary, • make sure you're too tired, • help you to oversleep or have other priorities every week, or • discourage you from joining your church family.
set new priorities for your life	• get you to maintain your old priorities, • make you fear change, • keep your focus off pleasing God daily, • tell you that it's not necessary to do so, or • tell you that none of what you read in this book is true.

Do you get the picture? Know that Satan will be there every step of the way to hinder you in your growing relationship with God. And he never leaves. As long as we're trying to live Christian lives—whether we're a newborn saint or have been serving God for a hundred years—Satan feels that he has a chance to win us over to his side. In reality, every Christian is *getting started with Jesus* every day.

Each day when we awaken, we face another day of choices. We choose how we will spend our time, how we will treat others, and how we will allocate our resources. Satan wants to influence each of those decisions, and he makes sure that we know it. So with Satan's voice so loud in our ears, how can we win this battle? Is it even possible? Not to worry. God says yes! With God, all things are possible (Matthew 19:26). Let's look at how we can win with God.

We must understand the battle

Battles are fought to achieve a goal. Countries fight one another for a variety of reasons, such as for not respecting one another's borders, to take land, or to stop injustice toward citizens. Corporations compete for customers and strive for market dominance. Lawyers face off in the courtroom to win verdicts in favor of their clients. Children get into scraps on the playground to gain or maintain respect. Christians have to battle Satan and our natural, human desires to attain the life that God wants for us and for our future generations.

You read earlier in this book about the three goals of Satan found in John 10:10, "to steal, kill, and destroy." We must never ever forget that. Those are Satan's goals every day of our lives. You also learned that sin (disobeying God) is inherent in us as human creatures. Galatians 5:19–20 gives us examples of how we would live if we acted on our natural desires. Satan battles us daily by tempting us to give in to our natural desires (e.g., sexual immorality, jealousy, drunkenness). Because not everyone has the same temptations and natural desires, Satan studies each of us to learn ours. Then he works to use them against us to achieve his goals for our lives. We fight to defeat him.

When we think of the word *battle*, we tend to draw images of physical combat involving the use weapons or fists. But our battle with Satan is spiritual, not physical. Here is how the battle is described in the Bible:

> For we are not fighting against flesh-and-blood
> enemies, but against evil rulers and authorities of

the unseen world, against mighty powers in this dark world, and against evil spirits in the heavenly places. (Ephesians 6:12 NLT)

Satan has an army of demons deployed across the earth to carry out his goals against mankind. It may sound like a science-fiction movie, but it is real. It's not crazy talk. Just think about it for a moment. Think about a big mistake that you made in your life. Consider why you did it. Did someone suggest it to you? Was it something that you felt you'd benefit from, even if you weren't sure that it was right—or even knew it was wrong? Might your life have been better if you'd made a different decision?

Here is a very simple example from my life. When I started college, I had a part-time job and was flooded with credit card applications. My parents provided me with a stable and secure life, but I worked for any extra things that I wanted. I liked to shop, so Satan didn't have to work very hard to lure me into the bondage of debt. My friends had credit cards and encouraged me to get them also (the temptation). We could shop and buy whatever we wanted (my natural desire). And that we did. I had nice coats, books, electronics, music, and so on. I bought nice gifts for people (pride) and really got caught up in unnecessary spending (poor stewardship) because I could pay later.

But, oh my goodness, did I pay later! I paid, and I paid, and it seemed as if the balances on my accounts would never go down. A friend told me that I didn't necessarily have to pay on time. It sounded like a plan. So I didn't. Then bill collectors called me and called the people that I listed as references looking for me. It was awful and stressful. It took me a decade to dig myself out of that hole. I'm getting stressed just writing about it! But you see how Satan used the tools of people and debt to entice my natural desire for stuff (feeding my greed and pride) to steal my peace, kill my joy, and destroy my credit history? He helped me do that to myself. That's the spiritual battle.

Before I got myself into that situation, I did not consult God or the counsel of my parents or people wiser than me (didn't fight).

Truth be told, I didn't want to. It sounded like a good idea, so I went for it. When I got to the worst place, like so many others, I consulted God. I received help and guidance from my parents, and I made many sacrifices and changes to get to a better state. Thank you, Lord!

We must arm ourselves for battle

I shared my story to give you an example of how Satan can lead us into dark places when we blindly follow his path and don't fight back. My example was getting into debt. For you or someone else, it could be sex, drugs, alcohol, crime, violence, infidelity, etc. We all have something that we need to fight against.

Let's turn our thoughts back to a physical battle and consider this: battles are mental before they are physical. Think about it. The decision to fight—the strategizing and coordinating—happens in the brain. Then what the brain imagines or formulates is executed in a physical manner. Sometimes the planning occurs well in advance of the battle; at other times, it occurs nanoseconds before each physical move. But the brain is in control. This is true of our physical conflicts and our spiritual battle against the evil within us and outside of us.

Because our battle against evil is spiritual, we need arms that work in the spiritual realm. Just as you wouldn't consider using your fist when fighting an enemy armed with an automatic rifle, you should not expect to win a battle against evil without the proper weapons. God has given us very clear instructions on how to equip ourselves for our spiritual battles:

> Therefore, put on every piece of *God's armor* so you will be able *to resist the enemy* in the time of evil. Then after the battle you will still be standing firm.
> Stand your ground, putting on the belt of *truth* and the body armor of God's *righteousness*. For shoes, put on the *peace* that comes from the Good News so that you will be fully prepared. In addition to all of these, hold up the shield of *faith* to

> stop the fiery arrows of the devil. Put on *salvation* as your helmet, and take the sword of the Spirit, which is the *word of God. Pray* in the Spirit at all times and on every occasion. Stay alert and be persistent in your prayers for all believers everywhere. (Ephesians 6:13–18 NLT; italics added)

Starting with the first verse of that passage, we read, "Therefore, put on every piece of God's armor so you will be able to resist the enemy in the time of evil." Remember that the enemy shows up for battle every day. This makes every day a "time of evil." Entering the world without being spiritually armed is like entering a battle in your underwear—not a good idea and not a strategy for victory. Unarmed Christians are easy prey for Satan.

Notice that the way to fight is to resist the enemy. That means don't give in to the temptation to do wrong. God tells us in James 4:7, "Therefore submit to [give in to] God. Resist the devil and he will flee from you." We will be strong enough to resist when we equip ourselves with God's armor.

The verse from Ephesians 6:14 says, "Stand your ground, putting on the belt of truth and the breastplate of righteousness." Jesus said, "I am the way, the truth and the life" (John 14:6). He also told us that Satan is the father of lies and that there is no truth to be found in him (John 8:44).

Satan attacks us with lies, hoping to tempt us to live in a manner that is not pleasing to God. We defeat him by accepting God's Word as true and by living to please Him (righteousness). Every time we are tempted but choose to do the right thing (as defined by God), we strike a blow to Satan.

Verse 15 reads, "For shoes, put on the *peace* that comes from the Good News so that you will be fully prepared [italics added]." What is peace? The dictionary defines it as "the absence of mental stress and anxiety" and "the state of prevailing during the absence of war."[10]

Satan attempts to attack us by stressing us out. Stress may be caused by fear, anxiety, pressure, burdens, relationship issues, and so on. But we can stand on God's Word and trust that He is in control.

He is aware of our situations, and He has complete power to handle them. Here is how we receive God's peace.

> Don't worry about anything; instead, pray about everything. Tell God what you need, and thank Him for all he has done. Then you will experience God's peace, which exceeds anything we can understand. His peace will guard your hearts and minds as you live in Christ Jesus. (Philippians 4:6–7 NLT)

God's Word also tells us in Romans 12:18 (NLT), "Do all that you can to live in peace with everyone." We can win against evil when we choose to love, forgive, and be merciful to others—even our enemies—as God has done for us.

Ephesians 6:16 reads, "In addition to all of these, hold up the shield of faith to stop the fiery darts of the devil." A shield is a piece of protective armor used to intercept blows.[11] To keep Satan's darts from penetrating our spirits, we must have faith that God is who He says He is in His Word. When we are facing challenges in life, Satan will throw his fiery doubt darts, with the hope of causing us to doubt God's existence, doubt God's presence with us, doubt His love for us, doubt His ability to help us, and doubt every other promise that God has made. If he can get us to doubt God, he can get us to seek alternative solutions—his solutions.

We fight back by believing God and by living with the faith that God is real, God is with us, God loves us, God is able, and God's Word is true. We must trust God all day every day and exercise self-control so that we can wait for His solutions to our needs through His guidance, answers, and provisions. We must not believe the enemy's lies or become so impatient that we take matters into our own hands. Our abilities are seriously limited, and although we can imagine what can happen tomorrow, we can only see the present. God has infinite vision, and He holds the future in His hands. We must place our faith in Him.

A remarkable thing about the shield of faith is how it enhances the power of other pieces of armor. For instance, it takes faith to activate the belt of truth. We must have faith in God to believe that His Word is true. We must have faith in God to experience the peace that only He can provide. We must have faith to accept Jesus Christ as our Savior. We must have faith for prayer to work. The shield of faith is reinforced and polished by the Word of God and as we witness His hand working in our lives.

Verse 17a tells us to "put on salvation as your helmet." A helmet protects our brains, the body's control tower. Without Christ, our brains are left spiritually unprotected, allowing Satan to move in to take control. When he takes control, he directs us to chase after things that lead him to victory. For example, he'll lead us to pursue wealth, material things, the admiration of others, and so on. He'll work to lead us into bondage, hoping that sin will become our helmet. He'll lead us as far away from God as he can with the intent of ultimately leaving us empty, broken, and bound for hell.

But when we accept Jesus Christ as our Savior, we put on the helmet of salvation. The Holy Spirit then moves into the control tower. Satan continuously hovers around the helmet, looking for uncovered or weak spots where he can get in. We can stand strong by trusting God completely, remaining faithful, and choosing to live by God's standards. When Satan suggests that we allow him inside the tower, we can fight back with the following words: "I am a child of God. I don't have to give in to this temptation. God takes great care of me and loves me like no one else can. He gives me strength, wisdom, and power to live right. I will live to please Him."

The second part of Ephesians 6:17 verse reads, "And take the sword of the Spirit, which is the Word of God." This is the only part of the protective armor that is a weapon. And what a weapon it is! It could have been described as a club to swing at things or a rock like David used when he killed Goliath, but God chose to describe His

Word as a sword—a weapon that cuts. And it isn't just any sword. Consider the following:

> For the Word of God is alive and powerful. It is sharper than the sharpest two-edged sword, cutting between soul and spirit, between joint and marrow. It exposes our innermost thoughts and desires. (Hebrews 4:12 NLT)

What a sword! Something else that's interesting about a sword is that it is a weapon used when under a close attack. We don't use a sword when our enemy is far away, but when he's within arm's reach—close enough to do us bodily harm. That tells us that God knows the enemy will be in our faces, launching spiritual attacks close enough to injure our bodies and souls. Notice that this weapon, God's Word, is the sword of the Holy Spirit. Let's read what Jesus told us:

> But the Helper, the Holy Spirit, Whom the father will send in My name, He will teach you all things, and bring to your remembrance all things that I said to you. (John 14:26)

Pay special attention to the words "bring to your remembrance all things I said to you." Remember that this is a spiritual battle in which Satan will attack you with his words. The Holy Spirit will bring God's Word to your remembrance to help you to conquer the enemy.

Jesus gave us a wonderful example of the Word in action in the fourth chapter of Matthew. He was just ending forty days without food and was hungry. Knowing that Jesus was physically weak and probably wondering how that might impact his godliness, Satan decided to tempt him. (If he's bold enough to try to tempt Jesus, he'll certainly try to tempt us.) Here's an encounter that shows Satan's words and Jesus's answer.

Satan's Offer	Jesus's Response
"If you are the Son of God, tell these stones to become loaves of bread" (Matthew 4:3 NLT). In other words, "Why are you hungry? Use your power unwisely to solve your problem and glorify yourself instead of God."	"No! People do not live by bread alone, but by every word that comes from the mouth of God" (Matthew 4:4 NLT). Jesus quoted Deuteronomy 8:3.
Then they went to the very top of a high temple, and Satan said, "If you are the Son of God, jump off! For the Scriptures say, 'He will order his angels to protect you. And they will hold you up with their hands so you won't even hurt your foot on a stone'" (Matthew 4:6 NLT). In other words, "Do something stupid. God will protect you!" Satan cleverly quoted a scripture this time.	"The Scriptures also say, 'You must not test the Lord your God'" (Matthew 4:7 NLT). Jesus quoted Deuteronomy 6:16.
Then they went to a very high mountain where Satan and Jesus could see all of the kingdoms. Satan said, "All these things I give You if You will fall down and worship me" (Matthew 4:9 NLT). No further explanation needed, right?	"Get out of here, Satan. For the Scriptures say, 'You must worship the Lord your God and serve only him'" (Matthew 4:10 NLT). Jesus quoted Deuteronomy 10:20.

Do you see how the Word works to destroy the words of the enemy? It will only work if you hear it or read it. We can't remember something that we never read or heard. This is why Satan tells us that the Bible is an ancient book that is no longer relevant. It's why he suggests that going to church and Bible classes aren't necessary. He doesn't want to empower the Holy Spirit within us. That way, his words will have more power. If we don't know God's Word, Satan can and will defeat us, and we may not even realize it until we begin to suffer the consequences.

Finally, we are instructed to "pray in the spirit at all times and on every occasion. Stay alert and be persistent in your prayers for all believers everywhere" (Ephesians 6:18 NLT). The importance of prayer was introduced earlier in this book. This scriptural passage shows us that it is an essential part of winning the spiritual battle. Through prayer, we keep the channel open to talk with God and to listen to Him through the Holy Spirit.

James 5:16 (NLT) tells us, "The earnest prayer of a righteous person has great power and produces wonderful results." Prayer is essential in battle. When we pray, things change for the better. When we stop praying, we open ourselves up to requesting and receiving counsel and direction from the enemy's camp, and things change for the worse.

Ephesians 6:18 also instructs us to stay alert. Another scripture, 1 Peter 5:8 (NLT), tells us why:

> Stay alert! Watch out for your great enemy, the
> devil. He prowls around like a roaring lion, look-
> ing for someone to devour. (1 Peter 5:8 NLT)

We stay alert by living with our eyes open and not blindly following the crowd. What is the enemy using to distract you? Is it a television program, a friend, an activity, or a song that puts wrong thoughts into your head or makes you believe that sin is acceptable? Is it an undesirable personality trait, such as a short temper, which Satan frequently picks at to lead you to misbehave? Is it a fear that Satan feeds to get you to do something that is detrimental to your life? Pay attention so that you can use your tools—faith, prayer, right and peaceful living, the Word, the Holy Spirit, knowledge of the truth, and confidence in your salvation—to fight and win.

The eighteenth verse closes with "be persistent in your prayers for all believers everywhere." The battle that we are in is not easy for anyone. We have to pray for the strength and effectiveness of all of God's people—our brothers and sisters through Jesus Christ. There should be no competition among us because we are working together toward the same goals: representing Christ in this world and drawing soldiers out of Satan's army into God's army. We are the Lord's human army—His boots on the ground. If one of us falls, we are to help lift the person up through our prayers, love, and support.

This chapter, no doubt, has given you a lot to think about. So give it very careful thought. Ask God to show you ways that the enemy has been fighting and winning in your life. Then review this information again as often as you need to in order to arm yourself to fight back. Become a trained, disciplined soldier by reading God's Word daily and praying about everything. Listen to our God, our commander, through our coach, the Holy Spirit. Stand on the truth of God's Word to become a Christian lie detector. Make the enemy mad by walking in peace and living right before God. To God be the Glory for giving us everything that we need to win.

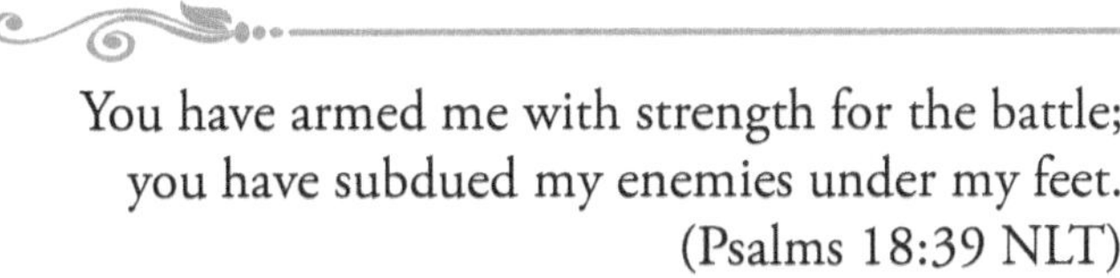

You have armed me with strength for the battle;
you have subdued my enemies under my feet.
(Psalms 18:39 NLT)

Chapter 10

Train Your Mind for Battle

My victory and honor come from God alone.

—Psalms 62:7 NLT

Before soldiers in our armed forces are sent out to battle, they go to live on a military base where they receive training and perform simulated exercises. Unfortunately, Christians don't have that luxury. As soon as Satan realizes that he has lost you, you become his enemy, and he launches his attacks. He figures that as a new Christian, you won't have the knowledge, strength, or courage to successfully fight back.

In many instances, he's right. That's why this book was written—to give you a head start. It's also why Christians who have been on the battlefield for a while feel compelled to share their experiences with you (and with one another) as part of your training. So consider this chapter as a battle-coaching session. In this chapter, you'll learn eight battle tips based on personal training, experiences, and observations.

1. *Know your issues and triggers*

Having decided to live in this world according to God's standards, Christians need to take a moment to identify the things we do that are not pleasing to Him (our sins). This isn't an activity that we engage in alone. We'll need to ask God for help. He doesn't reveal everything to us at once. He shows us some things now and others over time, as we learn and grow in our faith. As we get to know God and develop a true desire to please Him, he helps us see the areas in our lives that need fixing. This is a lifelong exercise.

Once we have identified something that is a barrier to developing a relationship with God, we must ask Him to help us to change. Then we must identify the triggers that lead us into that sin and strive to eliminate or avoid them.

Here's a personal example. As a teenager, I took delight in gossiping. I was spiritually immature and didn't realize the impact that it had on me or on others. When God showed me how hurtful it was through a personal experience and I saw where it was spoken against in His Word, I wanted to stop immediately. I no longer wanted to be that person or to be associated with people who talked about others for personal entertainment.

My trigger, I discovered, was talking on the telephone too much. Whenever I ran out of things to talk about, gossip would begin. I pulled away from the phone, had shorter conversations, and lost close friends in the process, but I became a better person. I'm still at risk of slipping up (people give you good stuff to talk about!), but Satan no longer uses me to spread rumors about others.

We will continue the exercise of identifying and managing our triggers throughout our lifetimes. We'll always have a desire to sin in various areas of our lives and will have to know this and avoid giving in.

2. *Guard the doors to your control tower*

Remember the helmet of salvation that you learned about in the last chapter? The helmet is a metaphor for knowing that you are protected by and through Jesus Christ. A benefit of salvation is that the Holy Spirit has moved move into your brain's control tower (your mind) to help protect you. Well, guess what, your control tower has doors that Satan tries to enter to take control. What doors? you ask.

These are your eyes, ears, nose, and mouth—access points for four of your five senses.

Satan desires to use something that you hear (such as gossip or sweet whispers in your ear), see (such as pornography), smell (such as a luring cologne or your favorite unhealthy meal), or taste (such as hard liquor or a tasty kiss) to activate your triggers or to develop new ones. So you have to pay attention and protect yourself.

The last of our five senses that is vulnerable to Satan's approach is the sense of touch, which we do primarily with our hands. We can think of touch as the knob that opens the door. When we touch something, information is sent to our brains. As you know, touch can be a strong trigger that can lead to interesting things (such as sex, alcoholism, fighting, and overspending). It is most often led by one or more of three other senses—sight, sound, and smell—and is the one that gets us the closest to sin. Consider this example from the Book of Genesis that you may be familiar with.

Adam and Eve lived the perfect life in the Garden of Eden. They had never sinned. When the serpent (Satan) asked Eve about eating fruit from the trees in the garden, she said, "It's only the fruit from the tree in the middle of the garden that we are not allowed to eat. God said, 'You must not eat it or even touch it; if you do, you will die.'"[12] She was armed with God's Word, which was the truth. Satan convinced Eve that God, the one who created her and had provided all her needs and the only Father that she'd ever known, was wrong—his weapon, a lie.

Once Satan's words entered Eve's ears and were processed by her brain, she neither challenged or resisted what she heard, nor did she hold firm to what God had said. Sound led to sight—"she saw that the tree was beautiful and its fruit looked delicious." Scripture doesn't tell us every step, but we can imagine that as Eve approached the tree, she was able to smell an attractive fruity fragrance. We read that sight led to touch ("so she took some of the fruit") and touch led to taste ("and ate it"). Eve sinned when she tasted the fruit.

You see, in this battle with Satan, we have to pay attention and guard our senses. This is why non-Christians feel that we *can't* do anything or have any fun. They don't understand that when we say no to certain activities or things, it isn't that we can't—or even that we don't want to—it's that we have chosen to protect ourselves by closing off an entry point for Satan. It's what parents do for their children when they don't allow them to watch certain movies or hang out with certain friends.

Be aware that Satan will always try to use what God gave you (physically and materially) to control you and cause you to behave in ways that lead to self-destruction.

3. *Challenge your feelings*

When we allow Satan to latch onto our senses and enter the control tower, he begins to whisper sweet nothings (literally) into our brains. His intent is to generate feelings and emotions that will lead us toward sinful behavior. When Satan gets into our heads, it is imperative that we engage all pieces of the armor that we are equipped with. He will serve up a lie, and it will echo in our heads. Therefore, we must counter it with the truth according to the Word of God. God has a Word for every situation that we may go through—every one! This is why it is important that we read the entire Bible so that our swords can be sharp to counteract Satan's attacks upon us. This means that we must read and meditate on scriptures daily and pray to God all day about everything.

Jesus Himself fought back with scripture. We can also. In the chart that follows are some common feelings that Satan will try to rouse in you. They are accompanied by several scriptures that can be applied to weaken the power of his attack.

We must avoid getting caught up in and taking actions based solely on our feelings. Also, we should be careful to avoid feeding negative thoughts and feelings. Doing so only gives Satan more power and increases the likelihood that we will make a wrong decision. Negative feelings toward ourselves can also lead to very serious results, such as clinical depression—even suicide. We must avoid the worst possible outcomes by trusting God and what He has told us in His Word.

When you feel	Apply God's Word
afraid	"So be strong and courageous! Do not be afraid and do not panic before them. For the Lord your God will personally go ahead of you. He will neither fail you nor abandon you" (Deuteronomy 31:6 NLT).
lonely	"And be sure of this: I [Jesus] am with you always, even to the end of the age" (Matthew 28:20 NLT)
worried	"Give all your worries and cares to God, for he cares about you" (1 Peter 5:7 NLT).
stupid	"If you need wisdom, ask our generous God, and He will give it to you. He will not rebuke you for asking" (James 1:5 NLT)
guilty	"If we confess our sins, He is faithful and just to forgive our sins and to cleanse us from all unrighteousness" (1 John 1:9).
angry	"And don't sin by letting anger control you.' Don't let the sun go down while you are still angry, for anger gives a foothold to the devil." (Ephesians 4:26–27 NLT).
sad or hopeless	"Weeping may last through the night, but joy comes with the morning" (Psalms 30:5 NLT).
defeated	"No weapon turned against you will succeed" (Isaiah 54:17 NLT).
lustful	"Run from anything that stimulates youthful lusts. Instead pursue righteous living, faithfulness, love and peace. Enjoy the companionship of those who call on the Lord with pure hearts" (2 Timothy 2:22 NLT).
arrogant or self-important	"God resists the proud, but gives grace to the humble" (1 Peter 5:5).

4. *Neither underestimate nor overestimate the enemy*

Up to this point, you may be excited to take on Satan, or you may feel that it'll be too hard and you can't fight. Well, in the Christian life, you'll tend to feel both ways depending on how experienced you are, how strong the battle is, and what else is going on in your life. But both thoughts are dangerous. Here's why.

When we underestimate Satan and decide that we will win all battles because we are strong and determined, Satan laughs at us hysterically. He knows that no matter how old we are or how long we've been a Christian, he is more experienced in this battle. Far more. He's been at this for thousands of years. He's seen every human personality type. He has taunted our ancestors and has known our family's tendencies and secrets. Just when we think we're strong enough to beat him, he digs deep into his trick bag and pulls out another clever approach.

Satan is patient and calculating—two things that we as humans often are not. He wants us to think that we can handle him because he knows that we'll rely less on God, and we'll be negligent about putting on our spiritual armor. He will get us, and we will fall very hard.

When we overestimate Satan and decide that the battle is too hard for us to fight, Satan does a victory dance. There is a great story in the Bible about David and Goliath. Goliath, a human giant who was part of the Philistine nation, taunted the nation of Israel, telling them to send a man to fight him. Whichever man lost, his people would become slaves to the other. All the Israelites were afraid, even their king, Saul. So they worried and talked about being defeated.

From a natural standpoint, they had no reason to believe that they would win. We feel this way many times in our lives. Situations of life will strike blows at us that will make us want to quit. One of the Israelites might have said "Forget this! Since we're going to lose anyway, I'm going to join the Philistine's army!"

Now David, who wasn't even in Israel's army, heard what Goliath said. When he saw that his king and army were scared stiff, he stepped up. He didn't step up because of his own power—he knew that it wasn't sufficient. He said, "The Lord who rescued me from the claws of the lion and the bear will rescue me from this Philistine!" (1 Samuel 17:37 NLT). And when the king tried to dress him in physical armor, David opted for his spiritual armor along with five smooth stones and a sling.

When Goliath saw this, he was offended. Israel had sent a child with rocks and a slingshot to fight him. Goliath thought his win was assured. David knew differently though. He told Goliath the following:

> You come to me with sword, spear, and javelin, but I come to you in the name of the Lord of Heaven's Armies—the God of the armies of Israel, whom you have defied. Today the Lord will conquer you, and I will kill you and cut off your head. And then I will give the dead bodies of your men to the birds and wild animals, and the whole world will know that there is a God in Israel! (1 Samuel 17:45–46 NLT)

David killed Goliath that day, and we are still talking about it and learning from it today. We must never forget that we are in a real battle, engaging with a real enemy. We must recognize that Satan is powerful. But we must always be aware that God has all power, and He is always in control. While it is wise to know our limitations, winning isn't determined by our limited abilities; it is determined by God's limitless power and might. God will fight your battles for you. Acknowledge the enemy, but put your trust, faith, and hope in God.

5. *When you fall, fall forward*

No matter how hard we fight, we will not win all the time. Doing so would require us to be perfect, and perfection is not to be achieved on this side of heaven. It is one of the ways by which God made us equal—we're all imperfect beings. Therefore, as Christians, we should spend our lives getting stronger, winning more, and losing less as time progresses.

Yet as imperfect people, we'll occasionally make choices that do not honor God. When we do, we lose a match with the enemy, and we face an important question: What do we do after we realize that we've made a wrong choice? Do we fall forward, or do we fall backward?

A sermon that my late pastor and father, Homer Gardner, gave on October 3, 2004, drives home this point. His message was, "One brief moment: a moment of pleasure, a lifetime of regret," during which he identified the seven stages of sin, each of which began with the letter *R*. They are illustrated in the following diagram in the fall-forward direction. The fall-backward steps are added for our purposes.

When we sin, we do so because we expect an immediate benefit. Sin often delivers. But it's short-lived. In order for sin to satisfy in the long-term, it has to be repeated. Repeating it leads to the bondage that Satan desires for us and exposes us to even greater and often irreversible consequences. The ultimate consequence is eternal separation from God and spending eternity in hell.

Continual sin leads to a wasted life with unnecessary problems, and it negatively impacts our children, their children, and those who are impacted by our lives. It prevents us from being in close relationship with God. It blocks our blessings and keeps us from having the abundant life and freedom that Jesus died for and desires for us.

When we fall forward, we recognize our wrong and make the decision and commitment to not repeat the action. In so doing, we choose the spiritual contentment, peace, and joy that God offers, instead of the repeated sins that leave us empty. Yes, we are guilty before our holy God, and we have to suffer consequences for our actions. But when we repent, we can keep moving forward.

Even though we may have repented, we can expect Satan to constantly remind us that we are guilty. He will tell us that we are not good enough for God and that He doesn't want us back. But we know that he's a liar, and we must believe the opposite.

T

Step 1: Rejection

I know what's right, but I decide to do wrong.

H

E

Step 2: Rebellion

My decision becomes my action.
I do the wrong thing.

F

Step 3: Rejoicing

A

I'm glad that I did it. I received
the expected satisfaction.

L

L

What happens next?

←**Backward**   **Forward**→

Step 4 (or 5): Realization		**Step 4: Realization**
"Maybe I shouldn't have done that."	C	"I really shouldn't have done that."
	O	
Step 5 (or 4): Repetition	N	**Step 5: Remorse**
"I plan to do it again and again!"	S	"I am sorry that I did it."
Eventually, in this life or the next…	E	**Step 6: Repentance**
	Q	"I acknowledge my sin before God, ask for His help to not repeat it, and honestly have no intent to ever do it again."
Step 6: Remorse	U	
"I shouldn't have lived my life that way."	E	
	N	
Step 7: Revelation	C	**Step 7: Restoration**
The choice of separation from God now leads to the result of separation from God in eternity.	E	"I accept God's forgiveness and, once again, choose to live a life that pleases Him."

Jesus died to cover our sins because He knew that we would be guilty. He did His part. Our part is to acknowledge our sin, dust ourselves off, accept the consequences, and keep our focus on moving forward with God.

6. *When tempted, look for the escape hatch!*

The late actor and comedian Flip Wilson had a routine that he performed often during many of his skits. After his character had done something wrong, he'd say, "The devil made me do it." It made viewers laugh because it poked fun at our human weaknesses since many people believe that they are powerless against Satan. The truth is that Satan cannot be blamed for our actions. He can only be blamed for tempting us. He knows our weaknesses and uses the right people and situations or both to tempt us. He knows that temptation is the starting point for sin and would like us to believe that flirting with sin is harmless. The Bible tells us the truth:

> But each one is tempted when he is drawn away by his own desires and enticed. Then, when desire has conceived, it gives birth to sin; and sin, when it is full-grown, brings forth death. (James 1:14,15)

For these reasons, it's imperative that we know our issues and triggers and avoid the people, places, and things that can lead us into temptation. Yet even when we are trying our very best, Satan invites us into sin. God, being our loving heavenly Father, knows this and has given us a fact and a promise in his Word:

> The temptations in your life are no different from what others experience. And God is faithful. He will not allow the temptation to be more than you can stand. When you are tempted he will show you a way out so that you can endure. (1 Corinthians 10:13 NLT)

As we try to live to please God and find ourselves tempted to do wrong, we must gain strength from knowing that we are able to make the right choice through God's power. When we find ourselves in a precarious position where the wrong choice appears to be the only option, we need only to look for God's way of escape—His escape hatch. It is there; we just have to muster the courage to resist sin and run away from the situation.

7. *Fight knowing the outcome will end in victory*

Many moviegoers enjoyed the *Rocky* series of movies. Although he was a good boxer, there were a few fights in which he would have viewers on the edge of their seats wondering if he would win. Often, just when it seemed that he would be defeated, he found the strength to get up and would emerge as a winner. If he had given up after his opponent won the first few rounds, he would have forfeited many of his victories.

It's very similar with us. Satan will attack us in clever ways and very often when we feel that we don't have the strength to fight. Satan will tell us that if God loved us, we wouldn't have to experience tough challenges. He'll tell us that living the Christian life is too hard and isn't worth it. He'll tell us that we're not strong enough to win against him. We must continually remind ourselves that he is a liar and that the truth cannot be found in him.

The real truth is that life is challenging for everyone. It is even more challenging for us because just as Christ suffered, we will have to suffer simply because we are His followers. We are not readily accepted in Satan's world. But there isn't a weapon that Satan can form to win against us when we live to please God (Isaiah 54:17). He can hurt our physical bodies and hurt our feelings, but he cannot touch our souls—the part of us that he really desires. God will fight for us and will never leave or forsake us. Isn't that awesome? He has told us that we are more than conquerors through Jesus, who loves us (Romans 8:37). This means that no matter what round we're in against the enemy, the outcome of the battle has already been determined—we are the winners. Hallelujah!

Yes, the battle will get hard at times. And we will not be victorious without receiving our share of battle wounds. But we are to lean on God by praying for his help and strength and filling our minds and spirits with His Word. He will give us the strength that we need. We gain strength by knowing that God is with us, and although we may be knocked down during a few rounds, we will win the battle.

8. *Take the testimonies of other Christians to heart*

The list of training tips can go on and on because Satan is clever, patient, and focused. Some of his strikes are directed toward Christians in general, and others are customized just for you. The tips offered in this chapter are tips that everyone can put to use. As Christians, we will continually learn from stories in the Bible, from the personal testimonies of those who have won and lost and from our own experiences.

We must listen, observe, reflect, and make sure that we put on our armor every day. If we live for God and keep our focus on pleasing Him, He will fight our battles for us, and we will win.

Physical training is good, but training for godliness is much better, promising benefits in this life and in the life to come. (1 Timothy 4:8 NLT)

Thoughts, Reflections, and Questions

Chapter 11

Live for God and Win!

*I have fought the good fight of faith, I have finished the race, and
I have remained faithful. And now the prize awaits me, not just
for me but for all who eagerly look forward to his appearing.*
—2 Timothy 4:7,8b NLT

When you think back on how much we've covered since you began
this book, you may feel that being a Christian requires quite a lot
from you. It does. It requires time, sacrifice, self-control, discipline,
and focus for a lifetime. You may be wondering if it's worth the effort.
You might ask, "Wouldn't it be easier to just believe in God and not
do any of what is shared in this book?" You wouldn't be alone in
asking that question. And unfortunately, too many Christians choose
that lifestyle. But while it might be easier, choosing that path will
cause you to miss the purposeful and blessed life that God desires
for you.

Consider this. When you are faced with an enemy *who can be
conquered*, it is faster and easier to surrender than to fight, right? But
if you don't fight, you miss out on the victory and the reward. Also,
think about how challenging it is to navigate through life. Which
decisions and paths are right for you? When should you choose one
option over another? You could figure it all out on your own, or you
can have your Creator help you every step of the way. Do you really
want to reject His offer?

Living to please God will be challenging at times. But it isn't challenging because God makes it so. It's challenging because of our natural desire to please ourselves and Satan's continual efforts to lead people away from God. We live in a world where living for God makes us different from a growing majority. But when we keep our focus on believing, trusting, and following Him, He makes it easier for us. God knows that when Satan wages war against His people, Satan's goal is to drive God out of us. Satan wants to rule this earth, and Christians are standing in his way.

We have to focus on winning with God and for God. Everything that you encountered in this book has been intended to help you to live as a winner through Jesus Christ. All of these—praying, reading the scriptures, listening to the Holy Spirit, putting God first, finding a church home, meditating and reflecting on the Word, arming yourself for battle, and training for battle—are to help you win. Satan knows that as we experience the feeling of victory on God's side, we'll become stronger, wiser, and more determined and effective followers of Jesus Christ.

What do Christians stand to gain?

When competitors face off in our physical world, there is usually a prize. For instance, wrestlers win a shiny large, wide belt. Olympic athletes compete for medals. Businesses win customers. But what do Christians gain? We live for God to go to heaven when we die, right? Many Christians and nonbelievers think that heaven is our only prize. Many may think that we lose in this life and win in the afterlife. But guess what, we win in this lifetime too.

Here is the first way that we win. When we were born, we had no record of disobedience. However, we are born with a natural tendency to sin. So as soon as we can think and act, usually as toddlers, we start doing bad things. Beginning with our very first sin, every time that we do something wrong, a sin is added to our records. Doing good deeds does not erase the sins on our records. There is nothing that we can do ourselves to clear our records. Throughout our lifetimes, Satan encourages us to sin more to have a better life. But sinning more leads to more negative consequences and a longer record of guilt.

Our sins separate us from God. If we die with a sin record, our spirits will suffer eternally in the place that God has prepared for Satan and those who have chosen to follow him. We'll be separated from God forever. That is a sad and hopeless state.

Wouldn't it be unfair for God to allow us to be born into such an environment and have no way of escape? God is not unfair. A key message in the Bible is that "God showed his great love for us by sending Christ to die for us while we were still sinners" (Romans 5:8 NLT). When we accept Jesus as our Savior, we are born again into God's family, and our sin records are cleared. Jesus took the punishment for our sins when He died on the cross for us. So we are released from having to carry records of guilt and shame. Thank you, Jesus.

Fortunately, Jesus's punishment continues to cover us, but it doesn't mean that we should freely sin. Sin has negative consequences and can still keep us from having a close relationship with God. Striving to live according to God's guidelines helps us to avoid repeatedly suffering from negative consequences. Living right helps us to win in this life. We'll never be perfect, and we will always need Jesus. But God will bless our efforts to obey Him and will help us to become increasingly stronger.

In addition to Jesus's payment for our sins, He also wants us to enjoy a good life. Let's read and memorize Jesus's statement below:

> The thief's purpose is to steal and kill and destroy.
> My purpose is to give them a rich and satisfying
> life. (John 10:10 NLT)

In the tenth chapter of the book of John, Jesus used the parable of the sheep and their shepherd. He was telling us that sheep know their shepherd's voice, and they follow him. The shepherd leads them, provides for them, protects them, and sacrifices himself for them. The thief, on the other hand, sneaks in, looking to draw them away from the shepherd and lead them to destruction. In this parable, the thief is Satan, and the shepherd is Jesus. Satan desires to lead followers of Jesus to destruction; Jesus wants to give His followers an abundant life.

And what does that abundant life look like? Below is a passage of scripture that many are familiar with, Psalms 23. It is presented in two translations, the traditional King James Version and the New Living Translation, which is expressed in modern English.

King James Version (most familiar)	New Living Translation
[1]The LORD is my shepherd; I shall not want.	[1] The Lord is my shepherd; I have all that I need.
[2]He maketh me to lie down in green pastures: he leadeth me beside the still waters.	[2] He lets me rest in green meadows; he leads me beside peaceful streams.
[3]He restoreth my soul: he leadeth me in the paths of righteousness for his name's sake.	[3] He renews my strength. He guides me along right paths, bringing honor to his name.
[4]Yea, though I walk through the valley of the shadow of death, I will fear no evil: for thou art with me; thy rod and thy staff they comfort me.	[4] Even when I walk through the darkest valley, I will not be afraid, for you are close beside me. Your rod and your staff protect and comfort me.
[5]Thou preparest a table before me in the presence of mine enemies: thou anointest my head with oil; my cup runneth over.	[5] You prepare a feast for me in the presence of my enemies. You honor me by anointing my head with oil. My cup overflows with blessings.
[6]Surely goodness and mercy shall follow me all the days of my life: and I will dwell in the house of the Lord forever.	[6] Surely your goodness and unfailing love will pursue me all the days of my life, and I will live in the house of the Lord forever.

You see, by choosing Jesus and living for Him, we are rewarded with a life of goodness, mercy, grace, and peace. We are protected, provided for, and wonderfully blessed. We get these benefits now—on *this* side of heaven. How wonderful!

Does this mean that we won't ever experience any problems in life? No, it doesn't. Life is hard at times for everyone—Christians and non-Christians, for God "makes His sun rise on the evil and on the good, and sends rain on the just and on the unjust" (Matthew 5:45).

We also live in a fallen world that is full of evil, sickness, and pain. But the Lord is our shepherd through our good times and our tough ones. He has told us that "all things"—including our hard times—"work together for good to those who love God, and are called according to His purpose for them" (Romans 8:28 NLT). This means that even our tough situations will eventually benefit us in some way.

We also win on this side of heaven when our Christian lifestyle draws people away from Satan and to Jesus Christ. When people observe Christians living differently and they see our love, joy, and peace, they'll become curious. They want to know our secret to happiness and will want to try it for themselves. This is our opportunity to tell them about Jesus. If they choose to believe and follow Him, He will welcome them with open arms. His blood will cover their sins, and He will become their shepherd. Satan will lose, and we will gain a new soldier for our team. Glory to God!

Finally, as if that isn't enough, when the Holy Spirit begins to produce fruit through us and we begin to reflect God's character, we help to create a better world. Those around us in our homes, work, community, and church families should enjoy interacting with us. Who wouldn't want to live with or near a person who shows genuine love, gentleness, patience, kindness, self-control, and goodness, and is joyful and peaceful? God makes a positive difference in this world through each of us. He uses our lives to bless others.

Do you see how much there is to win now? Do you understand why you should resist your natural desire to sin, resist Satan's temptations, and protect the abundant life that Jesus wants for you? I sure hope so!

A glimpse of heaven

There is much to gain in this life from living for God and having a relationship with Him. After our physical bodies have died and our earthly lives are over, we believe that God will gladly accept our souls into the place that Jesus has prepared for His people. Jesus told us the following:

> In my Father's house there are many mansions; if it were not so I would have told you. I go to prepare a place for you, I will come again and receive you to Myself; that where I am, there you may be also. (John 14:2)

The prepared place is described in the Bible as being constructed with radiant, precious stones and lit by the light of the Lord. Our limited minds cannot conceptualize such beauty, but we can imagine and long for this experience also described in that chapter:

> And God will wipe away every tear from their eyes; There shall be no more death, nor sorrow, nor crying. There shall be no more pain, for the former things have passed away. (Revelation 21:4)

In this life, there is crying, death, sorrow, pain, suffering, fear, and shame. Those feelings are part of the human experience because of our sinfulness. But God has a plan to give His people life in a place where those feelings and experiences are nonexistent. Imagine that.

When we live for God, there are benefits in this life and after it. He is with us now, and we will be with Him in the hereafter—a win-win situation. Glory be to God!

> But as it is written: Eye has not seen, nor ear heard, Nor have entered into the heart of man the things which God has prepared for those who love Him. (1 Corinthians 2:9)

A Final Prayer

Dear fellow Christian, you made the right choice in choosing Jesus as your Savior. I have shared what God has given me to help you get started in building a relationship with Him. Thank you for your time. This is only a foundation. God will teach you much more through His Word, His Holy Spirit, and through others who have been anointed and assigned to help you grow. We have a wonderful, caring heavenly Father who is eager to take your hand and lead you through life. He can be trusted to be everything that you need Him to be. He has great plans for you. He loves you with an unconditional, everlasting love.

God bless you and keep you. I am praying for you, and I wish you God's best.

> May the Lord bless you and protect you. May the Lord smile on you and be gracious to you. May the Lord show you his favor and give you his peace. (Numbers 6:24–26 NLT)

Acknowledgments

I give thanks to God, my Maker and Creator for giving me life, purpose, and for His love and great care for me.

I thank my dear husband, Anthony, for his love and continuous support of my goals and ideas. He always offers encouragement and shares his wisdom freely. I thank my children for their love and support.

I thank my dad and mom for training me up in the way that I should go. They were my first and most important examples of Christianity. I am still learning from them how to serve God through all stages of life. I thank my sister, Arrie, for her partnership as we have ventured into known and unknown territories. I thank my nieces and nephew for their hugs and smiles and for bringing extra joy to my life.

I thank the late Deacon Robert Thomas, who helped to confirm my call by directing me to Habakkuk 2:2–3. He encouraged me practically every week for at least three years to "wait on the Lord," assuring me that "it is coming." I don't mind waiting.

I thank my friends, Yvonne and Ed, who, in addition to my mom, graciously agreed to read the early manuscript and for sharing their feedback. I appreciate their time and encouragement.

It is my prayer that God will use this book to achieve its purpose in our lives.

Endnotes

1 Zacharias, Ravi. "What is Worthwhile Under the Sun?" Just Thinking. Ravi Zacharias International Ministries. Accessed 12/28/2011.

2 American Heritage Dictionary, Fourth Edition (2001). Dell Publishing. New York.

3 Note: Roman Catholic Bibles have an additional seven books collectively referred to as Apocrypha. They contain a variety of Jewish literature from the period between the Old and New Testaments. Source: Alexander, D. and Alexander, P. Editors, Eerdmans Handbook to the Bible. 1983. Michigan: Grand Rapids. William Eerdmans Publishing Co.

4 "Fast Facts from the Bible." Retrieved from http://bibleresources.bible.com/afacts.php.

5 Our Daily Bread is published by RBC Ministries. Order at www.rbc.org.

6 Today in the Word is a ministry of the Moody Bible Institute. Order at www.todayintheword.com.

7 YouVersion can be accessed at www.bible.com and in the app store of your cell phone.

8 The Apostles' Creed: The Old Roman Creed. http://www.spurgeon.org/~phil/creeds/apostles.htm.

9 Flynt, S. April 20, 2011. "Suicide Rates Rise in Poor Economy." WorldNow and WLBT. Retrieved from www. wlbt.com/Global/story.asp?S=14448816 on 5/28/11.

10 Dictionary! Caitlin Software, LLC © 2008–2010.

11 Dictionary! Caitlin.

12 Genesis 3:2–3 NLT.

About the Author

Olivia Jones loves the Lord and has a passion for sharing the good news of Jesus Christ. She serves her local church in Chicago, Illinois, where her husband, Anthony, is senior pastor. Her service has included designing and teaching adult and teen Bible classes, leading in the youth and music ministries, and playwriting.

Olivia has also authored *Fathered by God: Living Securely as His Beloved Child* and the companion *Living Loved Bible Study*. She believes that God has called her to "write the vision and make it plain" (Habakkuk 2:2) to help His children know Him, know why we need Him, and understand why we should live for Him.

Olivia has a bachelor of liberal arts from DePaul University, Chicago, and a master of business administration degree from Dalhousie University, Halifax. She is a wife, mother, grandmother, and committed servant of God.